THE SONG OF PRAYER

A PRACTICAL GUIDE TO LEARNING GREGORIAN CHANT

THE SONG OF PRAYER

A PRACTICAL GUIDE TO LEARNING

GREGORIAN CHANT

THE COMMUNITY OF JESUS

PARACLETE PRESS
BREWSTER, MASSACHUSETTS

2014 Second Printing
2010 First Printing

The Song of Prayer: A Practical Guide to Learning Gregorian Chant

ISBN: 978-1-55725-576-1

Library of Congress Cataloging-in-Publication Data

The song of prayer : a practical guide to learning Gregorian chant.
    p. cm.
  ISBN 978-1-55725-576-1 (pbk.)
  1. Gregorian chants--Instruction and study. I. Paraclete Press.
  MT860.S68 2009

    782.32'22--dc22   2009046187

10 9 8 7 6 5 4 3 2

Published by Paraclete Press
Brewster, Massachusetts
www.paracletepress.com
Printed in the United States of America

CONTENTS

✖

ACKNOWLEDGMENTS

CHAPTER 1
A BRIEF LOOK AT THE HISTORY OF CHANT
1

CHAPTER 2
˜ CHANT IS FOR EVERYONE
11

CHAPTER 3
PRAYING WITH THE BODY AS WELL AS WITH THE VOICE
17

CHAPTER 4
SQUARE NOTATION
21

CHAPTER 5
HOW TO READ AND SING CHANT NOTATION
29

CHAPTER 6
THE MODES USED IN CHANT
35

CHAPTER 7
THE DIVINE OFFICE OF COMPLINE
43

CHAPTER 8
CHANTING THE COMPLINE PSALMS—Mode 8
53

CHAPTER 9
CHANTING THE COMPLINE PSALMS—Modes 8g and 3a
63

CHAPTER 10
THE SHAPE OF THE MELODIC LINE IN PSALMODY
71

CONCLUSION
A LIVING CONVERSATION
75

NOTES
77

APPENDIX A
HOW TO PRONOUNCE LATIN
81

APPENDIX B
HOW TO DIVIDE LATIN WORDS INTO SYLLABLES
85

APPENDIX C
ANSWER KEY: MODES
89

APPENDIX D
ANSWER KEY: MARKING THE PSALMS
91

APPENDIX E
THE OFFICE OF COMPLINE
95

APPENDIX F
SELECT GLOSSARY
109

TRACK LISTING FOR ACCOMPANYING CD
111

ACKNOWLEDGMENTS

�֍

What is now known about the history and performance styles of Gregorian chant is due in large part to the scholarship of the Abbey of St. Peter, Solesmes, France. We are deeply thankful for their ongoing research, study, and commitment to the restoration of these "songs of prayer." The four Psalm antiphons in the service of Compline, may be found in the Psalterium Monasticum *(1981) and the hymn tune in the* Liber Hymnarius *(1983), both published by Éditions de Solesmes.*

✖

We gratefully acknowledge the scholarship and friendship of musicologist, Gregorian chant specialist, and Augustinian nun, Mary Berry, CBE *to whom we dedicate this book. Though she departed this life on May 1, 2008 (the Feast of the Ascension), her work will remain in perpetuity as a landmark for the study of the chant. Indeed, any who knew Dr. Berry and had the privilege of working with her know that her greatest desire was that the chant be "passed on."*

We at the Community of Jesus are grateful for her willingness to share her knowledge, enthusiasm, and love for the chant over many years. We happily offer this book to "pass on" that which we have learned from Dr. Berry and our own daily experience and study. We pray that it will aid you in your "song of prayer."

CHAPTER 1

A BRIEF LOOK AT THE HISTORY OF CHANT

The sacred universe
into which Gregorian chant introduces us
is the world of prayer—
or, if you prefer, of union with God,
which is the ultimate goal of prayer.[1]

—*Dom Jacques Hourlier*

✖

WHAT IS CHANT?

What is this thing called "plainsong," or as it is sometimes referred to, "plainchant," or "Gregorian chant," or simply "the chant"? In a nutshell, the chant is the unique music of Western Christianity and our closest living link with the church of the first centuries. In a broader context, it is truly the foundation of all our Western music.

"The chant grew originally out of the music of the Jewish ritual. The first Christians, themselves Jews, . . . brought into their worship the ancient Jewish custom of chanting aloud the books of the Bible. The melodies they used brought out the meaning of the words, made the text audible to a large gathering of people, and added beauty and dignity to the reading. In particular, the chanting of the psalms was to become the firm basis for all future Christian worship."[2]

Indeed, "the practice of singing psalms in the name of the Lord is observed everywhere," wrote Eusebius, the great church historian of the early fourth century. In pagan Rome, Christians were persecuted and often martyred, so they were forced to meet clandestinely in house churches and in the catacombs in order to pray together. A major aspect of their worship was the singing of psalms and other Scriptures. As Christianity spread among Gentiles, groups began to develop regular times throughout the day to assemble for prayer. This was one way of following the New Testament injunction to "pray continually" (1 Thessalonians 5:17).

During the following centuries, the practice of gathering for prayer several times a day continued—at first secretly during the periods of persecution, and then openly after Christianity became the official religion of the Roman Empire in the fourth century.

In the eastern part of the Roman Empire, Greek was the primary language. In the West, it was natural for the ancient prayers to be sung in Latin. As these times of prayer evolved, they came to be known as the Liturgy of the Hours, or the Divine Office. "Liturgy" comes from a Greek word for a public duty or service undertaken by a citizen. "Office" comes from the Latin word meaning "duty"—therefore "Divine Office" simply means "Sacred Duty." The terms "Divine" and "Office" recognize the Christian's sacred duty to pray continually.

WHO IS SAINT BENEDICT AND WHAT WAS HIS INVOLVEMENT WITH THE CHANT?

In Europe, numerous forms of the Liturgy of the Hours developed. In the sixth century, Saint Benedict wrote his *Rule*—a handbook for monks and nuns on how to live together in community. In the *Rule* Benedict prescribed a regular rhythm of life revolving around chanted prayer offices. Benedict's *Rule*, and his pattern of singing the chant offices spread throughout the West, leading to the establishment of hundreds of monasteries—and along with them, the widespread use of chant in worship. Though Benedict borrowed from earlier monastic practices, it was his form that would become the basis of all Western monastic prayer.

Few details are known about Benedict's life. He was born in Nursia (Italy) in about AD 480. He studied in Rome, where, confronted with the immorality and corruption of society, he decided to withdraw from the world and seek a life of dedication to God. For a time he lived as a hermit in a cave at Subiaco, but soon a community of men grew up around him. After a time, he moved with a small group of followers to Monte Cassino, where he remained until his death, sometime after 546. It was during his time at Monte Cassino that Benedict wrote the *Rule* for his followers.

Benedict's *Rule* stressed the ideals of the monastic life as it had evolved in the deserts of Egypt and Palestine, but tempered these with sensible and practical instructions designed to assist ordinary people in their pursuit of God. Two generations after Benedict's death, Pope Gregory I described the *Rule* as "remarkable for its discretion and its clarity of language." Benedict's knowledge and acceptance of human weaknesses led him to address such practical issues as food, drink, sleep, and work, as well as the spiritual virtues that should come to mark the life of each monk. In his organization of the corporate life of the monastery, he envisioned the community as a family in which the abbot served his fellow monks as a loving father, and they, in turn, learned to serve and care for one another.

The *Rule* set up a framework in which each individual could develop a daily relationship with God. Benedict planned a well-balanced schedule that divided the monastic day in this manner:

- the chanting of the psalms (*Opus Dei* in Latin, meaning "the work of God")
- manual work
- the study of Scripture and holy books.

Benedict left no question as to the hierarchy of these activities, stating simply, "Nothing is to be preferred to the work of God." This is evident in that he devoted twelve full chapters of the *Rule* (out of a total of seventy-three) to the chanting of the psalms.

THE MONASTIC DAY

As with everything else in the *Rule*, Benedict's rationale for the structure and content of each office was rooted in Scripture and in pastoral common sense. By following an ancient biblical practice of praying seven times during the day ("Seven times a day I praise you."— Psalm 119:164a), and once at night ("At midnight I rise to give you thanks."—Psalm 119:62a), those who followed Benedict's *Rule* recited the entire Psalter each week and still kept a balance between worship and manual work.

The Night Office, or *Matins*, was set in the middle of the night, while the Day Offices were spread more or less evenly throughout the daylight hours: *Lauds*, at daybreak, followed by *Prime, Terce, Sext, None, Vespers*, and, finally, *Compline* in the evening. Each of these times of prayer is commonly called an "office."

As precise as Benedict was in setting forth the schedule for the monk's day, he allowed for the possibility of each monastic house adapting the schedule to fit its own needs. This flexibility is part of the reason Benedict had such an enormous effect on religious and secular life over the ensuing centuries: it has allowed those who follow the *Rule* to adapt to various cultures and times.

In the second half of the twentieth century, Christians of many traditions wrestled with how to maintain the round of daily offices in the midst of the pressures of modern life and demanding ministries. Many modern monastic houses, including the Community of Jesus, have heeded Benedict's suggestion and have altered their schedules to better fit their own unique circumstances. By observing four offices a day (Lauds, Midday, Vespers, and Compline), we at the Community of Jesus keep the spirit of Benedict's *Rule* while realistically adjusting it to the demands of modern life.

THE FLOWERING OF CHANT

In the ninth century, Charlemagne joined various strands of spiritual practice—all having their roots in the ancient church—to help solidify his kingdom. Gregorian chant, as one of these strands, became a unifying force in Christian worship in an empire that included large portions of Western Europe. Although the Holy Roman Empire crumbled after Charlemagne's death, the form of chant that he promoted continued in practice throughout the West for centuries.

During these centuries, monks made two major contributions to chant. First, they organized the chants into an ancient Greek system of eight modes (we'll say more about modes in chapter 8). And second, the monks invented a way to write down the notes using elaborate markings called *neumes*—in some ways they resemble modern shorthand. The neumes represented the shape and the line of a melody.

The earliest chant melodies were simple, much as we would consider a children's hymn to be simple. When later chants were sung to more fluid and elaborate melodies, they still maintained their purity of form designed primarily to enhance the sound and emphasize the meaning of the words.

THE STANDARDIZATION AND CHANGE IN PERFORMANCE STYLE

For several hundred years, regional variations of the chant continued in what was primarily an oral tradition handed down from one singer to another. Then in the eleventh century, the Italian monk Guido d'Arezzo invented a system of lines and letters to portray the chant melodies. By the end of the twelfth century, square shapes began to be used to indicate pitch. When you look at sheet music or a hymnbook, you see that the music is represented by lines and notes. Modern music uses a later development of what Guido d'Arezzo invented.

Once chant music could be written down, using the newly invented line-and-square note system, the ancient neumes fell out of use. However, while the new notation could show pitches, as does modern musical notation, the system of lines and notes could not show the fluid nuances of rhythm portrayed by the ancient neumes. The oral tradition that had been handed down for generations began to die out and a heavier style of chant developed. This style came to be known as "plainchant," and remained the style for chant performance until the middle of the nineteenth century.

RESTORATION AND NEW INTEREST IN CHANT

In the 1830s, the young French monk Dom Prosper Guéranger reopened the vacant monastery of Solesmes in his hometown of Sablé, and charged his monks with the task of restoring chant to its former beauty. This restoration consisted of two primary components: the study of ancient manuscripts and the development of a lighter style of chanting where "words took on their true meaning, and the musical phrases recovered much of their natural suppleness and beauty."[3] By the 1850s, Solesmes monks were copying chant manuscripts from all over Europe. Carefully comparing manuscripts containing the ancient neumes to manuscripts containing lines and notes, they set about to determine how the chant would have been sung in its original form.

By the 1880s, Solesmes monks were printing chant books based on the old sources. For years, controversy raged between those who advocated "plainchant" and the Solesmes monks who advocated returning the chant to its expressive, ancient form. In 1903 Pope Pius X authorized the monks of Solesmes to prepare editions of chant for the Mass of the entire Roman Catholic Church, and during the next sixty years, the "Solesmes Method" of chant was taught throughout Europe and North America. Even as scholars debated the value of the Solesmes teachings, the recordings of the Solesmes monks became popular, and their books were widely distributed.

In the second half of the twentieth century, a deeper understanding of chant taught by Dom Eugène Cardine, a monk of Solesmes, brought about the publication of chant books containing both line and note music as well as representations of various forms of ancient neumes. These books allowed singers to read the melodies using the lines and notes, and yet grasp the subtle nuances of the chants portrayed by the ancient neumes. Before his death in 1988, Dom Cardine insisted that the restoration work should be ongoing, and that he was leaving it to his successors to continue the search for the truth and beauty contained in the ancient chants.

ADAPTING THE DIVINE OFFICE TO
A CHANGING WORLD

In the second half of the twentieth century, many churches, Catholic and Protestant, felt the need to reform and renew their liturgy, bringing it up to date with the needs of a modern world that had been devastated by two world wars. The renewal in the Roman Catholic Church took place under Pope John XXIII, who convened the Second Vatican Council (1962–65). Observers from Protestant denominations were invited to witness the events that took place.

As part of the overall renewal of the Catholic liturgy, the Divine Office underwent reforms in the wake of the Second Vatican Council. Much reflection went into the question of what material is needed to form an office. The council concluded that four elements were essential: a hymn, psalmody, a reading, and prayers. Under this wide umbrella, there is room to fit the particular needs of every community.

CHANT TODAY

In recent years, chant has had a rebirth in the church and, perhaps somewhat more astonishingly, among the general public! The world of music was startled by the sudden popularity of an album of chant, released first as a phonograph record and re-released by Angel Records as a CD in 1994. This CD was recorded by the monks of the Spanish monastery Santo Domingo de Silos. Entitled simply *Chant*, the album peaked at number three on the *Billboard* 200 music chart and was certified as triple platinum, making it the best-selling album of Gregorian chant ever released. Indeed, Gregorian chant as a form of church music has made a resurgence in the eyes and ears of the general public.

Other forces have also converged to bring the chant into the popular realm, as many people across the world who would otherwise have never known of the chant, are finding that the "sacred universe" into which chant introduces us really is available to them. Pope Benedict XVI has, from the beginning of his papacy, said that Gregorian chant has a very unique place in the life of the church, in the liturgy, and in sacred music.

The work of chant restoration continues. Throughout the world, numerous groups promote the singing of chant, including the scholas of the American choir, Gloriæ Dei Cantores, based at the Community of Jesus. While chant recordings are no longer reaching the triple platinum level, they continue to sell widely and steadily. In a world filled with noise, stress, and anxiety, the sounds of monks or nuns singing in a quiet church, filling it with ancient strains of praise to God can bring an otherworldly comfort.

However, as beautiful as it may sound, chant was not intended simply to be heard. The only way to fully explore its purpose and depth of meaning is to actively participate in it. People who offer their prayers using chant find themselves caught up in something much larger than themselves and are rewarded with unexpected fruit—just as Christians have been discovering for over 1500 years.

CHAPTER 2

CHANT IS FOR EVERYONE

When sung in Gregorian chant,
the prayer of the Church is supported
by the best music there is
for nourishing the soul, music which is also
an artistic masterpiece.[4]

—Dom Jacques Hourlier

✖

A DAILY RHYTHM OF PRAYER

P rayer chanted at various times spaced throughout the day provides a rhythm of prayer by which we offer praise to God and ponder his Word. The very act of chanting helps us lift our bodies and engage our minds in a way not common to everyday conversation. By taking time out of our busy day to keep this rhythm, we are reminded that the source and the meaning of our lives are to be found beyond the mundane tasks that otherwise define our daily schedules. Through these chanted prayers, whether we are alone or with others, we become part of a company of voices worshiping God.

An image sometimes used to describe the daily rhythm of prayer is that of a bridge between temporal time and eternity. The hours of prayer are the pylons that support this bridge and sustain the "traffic" that goes back and forth. When we engage in chant, we enter into eternal time and into Jesus Christ's presence in a particularly effective manner. In this way, we pilgrims, passing through this world, maintain a connection with our eternal home.

Even if we chant just one prayer each day, we join in the ceaseless round of prayer and praise that flows upward to God from every corner of the world. Even when we sing chant by ourselves, *we are never alone.*

PROTESTANTS AND THE LITURGY OF THE HOURS

Today, many Protestants sing the Liturgy of the Hours in some form as prescribed by Benedict.

In the sixteenth century, the rhythm of work, study, and prayer that characterized monastic life came to an end in the parts of Europe that were affected by the Protestant Reformation. Throughout these lands, monasteries were dissolved and seized or sold, and the monks and nuns often were forced to learn a trade and live "secular" lives.

Although the institutions that practiced chant were no longer in existence, the regular rhythm of prayer that they practiced continued.

In Germany, "[Martin] Luther embraced the Liturgy of the Hours as the prayer services of the whole church, laity and clergy alike. . . . Luther used the Daily Office as the foundation for his devotional life and his prayers."[5]

In Britain, the long tradition of the Liturgy of the Hours continued in the Anglican Church, and the offices were sung or said in English. The Book of Common Prayer incorporated the morning chant offices into the service of Morning Prayer, and the evening chant offices into the service of Evening Prayer. The office of Compline was renamed Night Prayer.

Several centuries after the Reformation, many Protestants felt called to return to formal monastic life. Despite a long period of prohibition, small groups of men and women formed communities that practiced Benedict's *Rule* while remaining in their Protestant denominations. Today, one can find Anglican Benedictine communities, Episcopal Benedictine communities, Lutheran Benedictine communities, and ecumenical Benedictine communities, such as the Community of Jesus. In one form or another, these modern communities observe the Liturgy of the Hours.

CHANT AT THE COMMUNITY OF JESUS

The Community of Jesus, Orleans, Massachusetts, is an ecumenical monastic community in the Benedictine tradition, which strives to hold in balance the values inherent in work, study, and prayer. Since its inception, the Community of Jesus has held as its primary vocation the worship of Almighty God. To that end, a regular rhythm of prayer in word and sacrament has evolved, including the Eucharist and the Liturgy of the

Hours. Members of the Community of Jesus gather several times a day for chant services, and we would like to use one of these services to help introduce you to chant—the office of Compline.

Compline is sung in the evening, completing the day and "putting the church to bed." Originally, Compline consisted of very simple and easily memorized psalms and prayers, so that before electric lights were invented, monks could sing this office in their dormitory with little or no light. It was not until later in the Middle Ages that the office was moved into the church, providing the possibility of illumination by a few candles.

Compline is part of the heritage of the universal church and the singing of Compline is a wonderful way to finish the day and prepare for rest. It's appropriate to chant Compline alone, but you might want to invite others to join you. You can sing with family or friends, such as a prayer group, a Bible study, a small group meeting, or a house church, and you can sing it in your home, church, or a place that works best for you. Wherever and with whomever you sing, you can be sure that you're joining with millions of others who are praising God, using the time-honored, beautiful sounds of chant.

CHANTING IN LATIN

After the Second Vatican Council, some communities kept the beautiful Gregorian melodies but substituted their own language for the Latin. The use of a modern language makes the texts immediately accessible to both singer and listener. However, because the melodies were created originally for Latin texts, they often needed to be adapted to fit the speech patterns of the modern language. Other communities elected to retain Latin for the Liturgy of the Hours. Still other communities chose to combine elements of Latin and their own language in their chant offices. The Community of Jesus belongs in this third category.

There are good reasons for continuing the use of Latin. For centuries, Latin was the language of worship in the West. While modern languages were developing, Latin was a constant presence in most of the Western church for more than a thousand years. Those who sing chant in Latin use the same words, and perhaps the same melodies, that have sustained worship for sixty generations of Christians. Those who sing Compline in Latin may well be chanting the same words and using the same melodies as Christians from the time of Constantine, the time of Charlemagne, the time of Saint Francis of Assisi, and the time of the Protestant Reformation.

Since the Latin words and the melodies were vitally linked, something is lost in this "marriage" if one of the partners were to change identity: it would no longer be the same union, and therefore it would no longer convey the meaning in the same way.

Reformers, such as Thomas Cranmer in England, Jean Calvin in Geneva, and Martin Luther in Germany, favored changing to the common dialects of their respective countries. Adopting the native language of a people, whether English, French, or German, was an important element of the Reformation, because for the first time it made the offices understandable to the laity who no longer knew Latin. Now, five centuries after the Reformation, many Protestants are rediscovering the value of singing Gregorian chant as it was originally written. When we chant the ancient texts, we are united with others who speak a different modern language but incorporate Latin in their worship. The choice to use Latin in worship is made, not to preserve Gregorian chant as a museum exhibit for the modern world, but rather to plunge ourselves into a current of prayer and praise that will help to transform us.

✂

No matter which language is used for the Liturgy of the Hours, Christians continue to enjoy this ancient and beautiful song of prayer to offer praise to God.

Before you read the next chapter, please take time to listen to the Compline office on **TRACK 1** *of the CD that accompanies this book—it's about fifteen minutes long. The words and music for the office of Compline are given in Appendix E, but we encourage you to just listen to it first.*

CHAPTER 3

PRAYING WITH THE BODY AS WELL AS WITH THE VOICE

Both the Hebrew and the Christian Scriptures tell us that true worship involves the whole person—the body as well as the mind and heart. In other words, there is meaning in what we *do* as well as in what we say.

When we sing chant in Latin, we have plenty to keep our minds occupied: singing the melodies of the psalms, pronouncing the Latin words properly, and trying to understand the meaning of what we are chanting. At the same time, our bodies can also be fully involved in several ways, through various postures and gestures. Our bodies carry and express the prayer and aspirations of our hearts, much as a hug can say "I love you" more effectively than words alone.

BOWING

In every office there are specific points when it is traditional to bow. These include any time we acknowledge the Holy Trinity with the words *Glória Patri, et Fílio, et Spirítui Sancto* (Glory be to the Father, and to the Son, and to the Holy Spirit). This happens in the opening of the office and at the end of each psalm: we bow as we sing those words, and we come back upright at the words *Sicut erat in princípio* (as it was in the beginning . . .).

Likewise, we bow during the final verse of the hymn, when extolling the Father, Son, and Holy Spirit. We also bow during the Lord's Prayer, rising up again at the words *Et ne nos indúcas in tentatiónem* (and lead us not into temptation). We bow again during the collect (a short prayer at the end of the service).

If you are singing the office of Compline in a church, you might consider opening and closing the office by bowing toward the altar out of reverence for God, and, if others are singing with you, you may follow this by a half bow to the other person(s), as a sign of reverence for the presence of Christ in them.

THE SIGN OF THE CROSS

So that we may all begin the office in unison—with one gesture as well as with one voice—as we chant the opening versicle, <u>*Deus*</u> *in adiutórium* <u>*meum*</u> *intén̄de* (O God, come to my assistance), we make the sign of the cross: the four underlined syllables are the moments when we touch our forehead, our heart, our left shoulder, and then our right shoulder.

The sign of the cross is an ancient gesture. As far back as the third century, there is evidence that Christians "sealed" themselves on the forehead with this sign, both as a symbol of mutual recognition in times of persecution and as a way of sanctifying themselves and the activities of daily life. Soon thereafter, the sign of the cross was employed at both baptism and confirmation, symbolizing a seal of ownership, by which the candidate was reminded that he or she belonged to God. As a liturgical action, this sign came to be used for the blessing of both persons and things. Later, the simple gesture of making the sign upon one's forehead developed into what we now know as the tracing of the cross upon our bodies.

SITTING AND STANDING

We begin and end the office standing. Standing is a sign of reverence to God. As shown in paintings on the walls of the catacombs in Rome, the early Christians used to pray standing, with their arms uplifted. Although less familiar to us, standing was, for many centuries, the usual posture for communal prayer, and it is still the norm in Eastern Orthodox churches. In the Liturgy of the Hours, following the antiphon and intonation of the first half of the first psalm verse, we sit for the psalm. We stand again after chanting the first half of the last verse of each psalm, and bow for the *Glória Patri*. Through all of these gestures, we are, as creatures, paying homage to God, our Creator, and to his majesty, and thus the gestures carry a weight of meaning far beyond the actual motions we make.

If we remind ourselves of the significance of what we are doing and fully enter into it, these actions will add another dimension to our worship. They will, in turn, shape us. As George Guiver, superior of the Community of the Resurrection in Mirfield, England, put it: "The world is real, and prayer is real. If both are brought together, both will be more real still. . . . It is therefore inevitable that Christian prayer, no less than Christian service, will demand a living-to-the-full of the incarnation. . . . We cannot be human this side of the veil without our body, and neither can we be Christian. . . . It is a great mistake to believe we can leave our body out of prayer."[6]

✖

Now that we have looked at some of the history of the chant, and some of the mechanics accompanying it, we will learn how to sing it.

CHAPTER 4

SQUARE NOTATION

✖

In this chapter, we will learn how to start singing chant. To begin, we will look at the musical notes used in chant. Using lines and notes to represent music is called *notation*. When we look at any piece of chant, we immediately notice that the music looks different from modern music. The chant notes, known as *square notes*, were invented in the twelfth century and developed in later centuries.

Listen to **TRACK 2** on the CD—you are listening to one of the Compline antiphons, *Salva nos.* The musical notation for this antiphon is on the next page. As you listen, look at the antiphon. Hear how the tune follows the line of the music you are looking at. Now try to sing the antiphon with the CD.

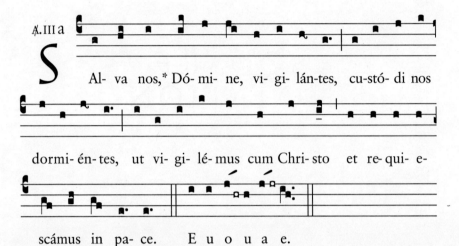

(See *Select Glossary* on page 107 for the meaning of the letters following the antiphon.)

Save us, Lord, while we keep vigil; keep us while we sleep,
that we may watch with Christ and rest in peace.

The scribes who wrote out the notation used quill pens with square tips and, depending on the angle at which they were holding the implement, they were able to make the shapes that we see in the piece of chant above.

The square notes are placed on four lines that go horizontally across the page. We call these lines a *staff*. In modern music, the staff has five lines. Most chant pieces have a moderate range of notes, and so a staff with only four lines is used.

NEUMES

There are various types of chant signs, or notes, called *neumes*. The term *neume* refers to all the notes that are sung on a single syllable of text. Where there are many notes on a syllable, these notes can be broken down into combinations of smaller elements of one, two, or three notes. This makes it simple to learn chant, because all we have to do is learn these fundamental patterns.

Although we don't have to know the names of each neume in order to sing the chant, we offer them here so that you may come back and learn more details later. It's more important to learn what the notes *do* than what they're called.

The names given to the individual notes (shown in parentheses below) come from Latin and Greek. In many cases, they describe either the actual shape or the function of the sign. For example, the two-note neume that starts on the lower of the two notes is called a *pes*, which is Latin for "foot."

One-Note Neumes

There are two types of neumes consisting of one note. Both are single squares, one with a tail and one without. Both are sung exactly the same way, and they represent a single pitch.

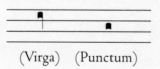

(Virga)   (Punctum)

Two-Note Neumes

There are three types of neumes consisting of two notes. The first type begins on a higher note and moves to a lower note. The second type begins on a lower note and moves to a higher one. (Notice that if the notes are stacked directly over each other, the lower one gets sung first.) The third type repeats the same note. This *repercussion* is sung by lightly pulsing the two notes.

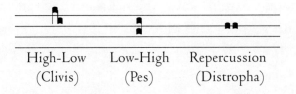

High-Low   Low-High   Repercussion
(Clivis)   (Pes)   (Distropha)

Three-Note Neumes

Three-note neumes make more combinations possible. The order of notes is read from left to right. The *high-low-high* is characterized by its sweeping pen stroke. The first and second notes of this neume are found at the highest and lowest points of the stroke. In the example given below, the first note would be on the top space and the second note would be on the middle space.

The *low-high-low* combination is straightforward and easy to identify, as is the *low-to-high* combination. The diamond-shaped notes of the *high-to-low* are normally sung at the same speed as single square notes, though perhaps a bit lighter. Their unique shape was made from the angle at which the scribe held his quill.

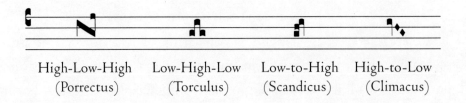

High-Low-High   Low-High-Low   Low-to-High   High-to-Low
(Porrectus)   (Torculus)   (Scandicus)   (Climacus)

Special Signs

In addition to the basic notation, there are also a few special neumes as well. One is called a *quilisma* (quill-LIZ-muh). In the pattern below, notice that the middle note is indicated with a zigzag pattern. This design distinguishes it from the other notes, and as its shape might suggest, it is an energy note. These three notes are sung in a very specific way: you lengthen the first note, energize quickly through the second note, and head for the top note, which is also lengthened.

Any note or series of notes can be slightly lengthened by adding a line over them. This line is called an *episema*. We usually find a dot on notes before a full or double bar. Keep in mind that each of these symbols makes the note just a *little* longer. Remember that chant is based on speech rhythm. We want to treat these lengthenings in the same way that we would pause or stop if we were speaking the text.

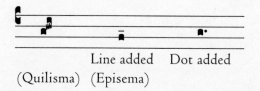

     Line added Dot added
(Quilisma) (Episema)

Another special form of neume is called a *liquescent* (lih-KWEH-cent). In the example on the next page, you will notice that the second note has a little tail. That small note indicates that more attention is to be given to a particular consonant—usually an *l*, or an *m*, or *n*—by almost a hum on that pitch. For this reason, some people refer to these notes as "humming notes." The word *hosanna* is often sung using a liquescent. The little note coincides with the *n* of the middle syllable, so we actually make that sound on that pitch before releasing to the *na* of the final syllable.

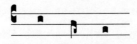

Ho- saN- na

CLEFS

In Western music, the treble clef and the bass clef are used in modern musical notation. Similarly at the beginning of each line of Gregorian chant, we also find signs known as *clefs*, only these signs look different from the treble and bass clef signs. The clef signs used in chant tell us that DO or FA (the names of pitches) is located on the particular line that the clef encompasses. (We'll look at the meaning of DO and FA in more detail later on.)

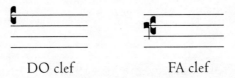

DO clef   FA clef

In modern musical notation, a note on the staff always represents the same pitch. In chant, however, the pitch of an individual note can move up or down relative to the position of the clef.

QUARTER, HALF, AND FULL BARS,
AND THE GUIDE

Chant has its own kind of musical punctuation similar to the punctuation that we use in writing. A *full bar* is often used to show the end of a sentence. A *double bar* acts as a full bar at the end of a chant. A *half bar* might be found at a mid-point, such as at a colon or a semi-colon. A *quarter bar* could be found at a comma or sometimes just in the middle of a sentence. In the interest of keeping the chant line moving, we do not pause at a quarter bar if there is no punctuation indicated in the text, but we usually do pause for a breath at half and full bars.

Notice the very small note at the end of each staff of chant. This *guide note* (called a *custos* [KOOSE-tohss]) is used to identify the first note of the next staff. It is not sung, but it is a great aid to finding your next pitch as you move down the page from one staff to the next.

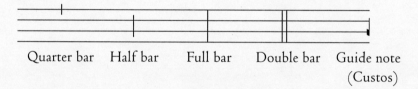

Quarter bar   Half bar   Full bar   Double bar   Guide note
                                                      (Custos)

Now look back at the piece of chant at the beginning of this chapter, and see how many of these chant elements you can identify.

CHAPTER 5

HOW TO READ AND
SING CHANT
NOTATION

✖

RELATIVE PITCH

As we mentioned in the last chapter, one of the differences between square chant notes and modern musical notes is that square notes represent *relative* pitch, while modern notes represent *absolute* or fixed pitch. If, for instance, you play middle C on a piano, it will sound a certain pitch. If that note were played on another instrument, say a flute or a violin, it would be the same pitch. Every note written on the modern staff corresponds to a certain fixed pitch. However, this is not true with chant notes. The purpose of chant notes is to show us the *relationships* between the pitches, not the pitches themselves. You can pick any starting pitch that is comfortable for you, and then sing the rest of the notes relative to that one. The starting pitch might be higher or lower, depending on what you, the singer, decide.

Here's one way to understand what relative pitch means: Try singing "Mary had a little lamb"—pick a note, and sing the words. Now start higher, and sing these same familiar words. Then start lower and sing the same words. You will find that you automatically adjust the notes to make the tune work, no matter where you start. We do the same thing with chant.

The best tool we have for working with a relative system is the *solfège* system. Solfège (a French word pronounced much like "SOUL-fedge") involves using the syllables DO-RE-MI-FA-SOL-LA-TI-DO for the pitches. Many of us are familiar with these names from Julie Andrews's rendition of "Do, a Deer" in the movie *The Sound of Music*, made in 1965 by Twentieth Century Fox. This popular song taught us the syllable names and their order, but they have actually been in use since the eleventh century. You will find that solfège makes things much easier as we learn to chant.

CLEFS

In the last chapter, we saw the two clefs that are used in chant. The following examples show how the clef signs help us identify each note on the staff. In the first example on page 31, the DO clef sign shows that the top line is DO. The space right under that is TI, followed by LA on the second line down. If we continue down through SOL, FA, MI, and RE, we end up with DO again, located on the bottom space.

It is helpful to learn to say the solfège names from bottom to top as well as from top to bottom.

In the second example, FA is indicated by the FA clef sign on the third line from the bottom. This time you have to count both up and down from that third line.

DO TI LA SOL FA MI RE DO

LA TI DO RE MI FA SOL LA

Now you may want to try it yourself. In the blank staff below, starting on the bottom line, make a square note for each consecutive line and space, heading in an upward diagonal to the right. Then write the solfège names underneath each note. Hint—the bottom line will be FA. (After you try this, check your answer against the Answer Key in Appendix C.)

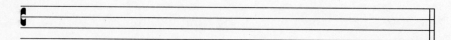

THE HALF STEP

Perhaps even more important than identifying the various notes, the clef identifies where the half steps lie in the scale. The importance of the half step will become clearer in the next chapter. But for now, we just need to become familiar with what a half step is and where to find it.

Western music is based on a system of whole steps and half steps. The smallest difference between two consecutive pitches is a half step. And, as you may have guessed, two half steps equal a whole step. One way to visualize these steps is to think of a piano keyboard.

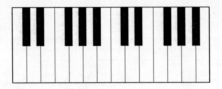

Imagine two white keys with a black key between them. The distance from either white note to the black note is a half step, while the interval between the two white notes is a whole step. There are places on the keyboard where there are two white keys together without a black key between them. The interval between those particular white keys is also a half step. If this sounds confusing, don't worry. Your musical intuition can guide you through half and whole steps.

Now it is time to sing a scale, going from DO to DO. Listen to **TRACK 3** on the CD and sing along with the cantors. While you are singing, look at the diagram on the following page, and you will notice that the half steps, marked with a caret, or pointed top, come between MI and FA, and

TI and DO. Do you know that you have just sung five whole steps and two half steps? Your ear knows a lot about music! The half steps always fall between MI and FA and between TI and DO. All the other intervals are whole steps. Try singing the scale again while looking at the diagram. Then try singing it in the other direction, from highest note to lowest note, using the solfège names. Again, you may find the CD helpful.

1 step	1 step	½ step	1 step	1 step	1 step	½ step
DO	RE	MI	FA	SOL	LA	TI	DO

Remember that we said the clef sign would help us identify where the half steps are in the scale. The half step always lies just below the FA and the DO.

Now you may want to launch out on your own. Look at the following example. You will want to pick a comfortable note to begin with, then sing the scale. As you go up the scale, point out to yourself where the half steps are, between MI and FA and TI and DO.

Let's try a few different combinations using the following example. Point to the pitches as you sing them:

DO RE MI FA SOL LA TI DO

Try DO-TI-DO (the top note of the scale, the note right below it, back to the top note). Sing it on your own, and then sing along with **TRACK 4** on your CD. Don't be surprised if the pitch you chose is slightly

different from the one the cantors use. Remember, chant uses a relative
system. The important thing is to sing a half step between DO and TI.

Now try DO-TI-LA-TI-DO followed by DO-LA-DO. Use TRACK 5
of the CD if you need to. If you get confused, just come back to whatever note you picked for DO and start over again.

Here's the next challenge. Look at the next example, going from FA
to FA. Locate the half steps between TI and DO and MI and FA, and
mark them with a caret (^). Now try singing a scale going from FA
to FA, making sure you sing half steps where you have them marked.
This is not going to sound like the DO to DO scale. Sing along with
TRACK 6 on the CD several times.

FA SOL LA TI DO RE MI FA

(After you mark the half steps, check your answer against the Answer
Key in Appendix C.)

Gregorian chants are melodies based on a series of half steps and
whole steps. Identifying, hearing, and practicing half and whole steps
will give you a musical foundation for learning to chant.

CHAPTER 6

THE MODES USED
IN CHANT

✖

HOME TONE AND RECITING TONE

I n the last chapter we looked at the scale from DO to DO. The half
steps fall between the third and fourth notes (MI and FA), and the
seventh and eighth notes (TI and DO). In the example below, mark
the half steps with a caret (^). You might want to review the sound of
this scale by singing along with the CD, **TRACK 3**.

DO RE MI FA SOL LA TI DO

(After you mark this scale, check your answer against the Answer Key in
Appendix C.)

This is known as the major scale, and much of Western music is built on it. We call DO the root or *home tone*, because the scale is based on and begins with that note. Now try singing down the scale, starting from the top DO, but on the way down stop on RE. Does that sound finished to you? It should only sound finished when you sing the final DO. We recognize this major scale sound without even realizing it, because it is so much a part of our culture and musical heritage.

But what about Gregorian chant? Chant is not based on the major scale. Rather, it is based on different scales with various home tones. These different scales are called *modes*. Let's look at the next example to see what happens if we start the scale on RE and make it the home tone. The half steps are still between MI and FA, and TI and DO, but with our new RE scale, these half steps fall between the second and third notes, and the sixth and seventh notes. Place a caret mark between the half steps below and then try singing this scale, taking special care with MI and FA, TI and DO. Listen to the CD, **TRACK 7**, and sing along with it to check yourself.

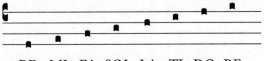

RE MI FA SOL LA TI DO RE

(After you mark this scale, check your answer against the Answer Key in Appendix C.)

This scale sounds different from the major scale because the half steps are between different degrees in the scale. This rearrangement is what gives the mode its unique sound. The RE modes have a particularly haunting sound of great beauty.

In Gregorian chant we use modal scales based on RE, MI, FA, and SOL as the home tones. If you are feeling particularly adventuresome, try singing a scale based on MI, then FA, and finally SOL. First, check where your DO clef sign is, and then mark the half steps with carets, noting where they appear in these modal scales. For example, in the MI mode, the half steps are between the first and second, and fifth and sixth degrees of this particular scale. Listen to these on the CD, and sing along with the cantors.

MI Scale   **TRACK 8**

MI FA SOL LA TI DO RE MI

FA Scale   **TRACK 6**

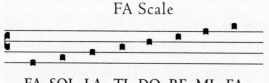

FA SOL LA TI DO RE MI FA

SOL Scale   **TRACK 9**

SOL LA TI DO RE MI FA SOL

(After you mark these scales, check your answer against the Answer Key in Appendix C.)

There is another important pitch in every mode: the *reciting tone*. This pitch is most easily identified when chanting the psalm verses because it is the note on which we recite most of the text. We will learn more about this later.

THE EIGHT CHURCH MODES

When we use the word *mode* in common speech, we often use it to mean "a manner or way of acting, doing, or being." In music, we sometimes refer to "major modes" and "minor modes" as ways of indicating two different forms of the arrangement of the musical scale. In chant, however, the word *mode* refers to the selection and arrangement of the whole steps and half steps in a scale.

The modes as we know them evolved gradually over the centuries. It was after the ninth century that music theorists organized the various chants into a system of what are now called "the eight church modes." Each mode is characterized by a certain home tone and a certain higher-pitched reciting tone. This unique combination of home and reciting tones, with its positioning of half steps, is what gives each mode its different sound and character. Generally speaking, the pitches in a chant melody fall between the home tone and the reciting tone of the mode. That is why it is so helpful to be able to sing the modal scale: it gets you "in the right mode."

There are pairs of modes that share the same home tone:

Modes 1 and 2 are RE modes
Modes 3 and 4 are MI modes
Modes 5 and 6 are FA modes
Modes 7 and 8 are SOL modes

The Home and Reciting Tones with Musical Examples for Each of the Eight Church Modes

Mode 1

Home tone: RE
Reciting tone: LA

RE LA

(LA)   (RE)
Ký-ri- e   e-   lé- i- son.

TRACK 10

Mode 2

Home tone: RE
Reciting tone: FA

RE FA

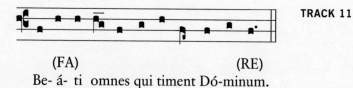

(FA)   (RE)
Be- á- ti omnes qui timent Dó-minum.

TRACK 11

Mode 3

Home tone: MI
Reciting tone: TI

MI TI

(TI)   (MI)
Ký-ri- e   e- lé- i- son.

TRACK 12

Mode 4

Home tone: MI
Reciting tone: LA

TRACK 13

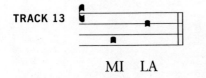

MI LA

(LA)   (MI)
Fi-dé-li- a óm-ni- a mandá-ta e-ius:

Mode 5

Home tone: FA
Reciting tone: DO

TRACK 14

FA DO

(FA) (DO)
In conspéctu an-ge-ló-rum

Mode 6

Home tone: FA
Reciting tone: LA

TRACK 15

FA LA

(LA)   (FA)
Be-ne-dícam Dóminum   in om-ni témpo-re.

Mode 7

Home tone: SOL
Reciting tone: RE

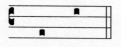

SOL   RE

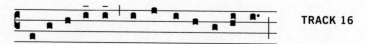

TRACK 16

(SOL)   (RE)
In pa-ra-dí-sum de-dúcant te án-ge- li:

Mode 8

Home tone: SOL
Reciting tone: DO

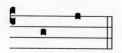

SOL   DO

TRACK 17

(SOL)   (DO)
Magní-fi- cat   á- ni-ma me-a Dó-mi-num.

CHAPTER 7

THE DIVINE OFFICE OF COMPLINE

Save us, Lord, while we keep vigil;

keep us while we sleep,

that we may watch with Christ

and rest in peace.

—Compline antiphon

✘

In this chapter, we're going to tell you more about the office of Compline to help you learn to pray in this ancient song of prayer.

COMPLINE: "PUTTING THE CHURCH TO BED"

The texts and tunes for each of the offices vary according to the seasons of the church year and certain saints' days. Compline is the one office that, for the most part, remains the same throughout the church year. Its quiet, comforting rhythm has led many to describe Compline as "putting the church to bed." It is the most meditative office of the day, and it is the favorite of many people who sing chant.

With our ability to turn on electric lights at the flip of a switch, much of the association of night with fears and terrors has faded away. Yet, darkness still creates a sense of fear. We may feel threatened by something outside that we cannot control or by something inside that feels overwhelming. At times darkness looms large. Through this brief song of prayer, we call out to God for his protection and ask for his angels to watch over us. We pray, with the words of Psalm 91, for God to cover us with his wings. We are reminded again that he will satisfy us with good things.

Sleep reminds us of our final sleep in death. We begin the office by confessing our sins to God so that we may end our day and begin the night in the assurance of his mercy and forgiveness. We chant Jesus' own words to the Father, "into your hands, [Lord,] I commend my spirit," and we pray that whether we wake or sleep, we may live with him.

As we recall Simeon's words when he held the infant Jesus in the temple, "For my eyes have seen your salvation," we remember that we too have seen the face of Jesus in the events of the day, and we ask him to grant us his peace. We make the confident prayer of the psalmist our own, closing the work of the day: "I will lie down and sleep in peace, for you alone, O Lord, make me dwell in safety."

THE ELEMENTS OF COMPLINE

In this chart that shows the elements of Compline used at the Community of Jesus, you will see how Latin and English are interspersed:

Opening sentences (Latin)

Confession and Absolution (English)

Hymn (Latin)

3 psalms with an antiphon (Latin)

Scripture reading (English)

Versicle and Response (Latin)

Canticle *Nunc Dimíttis* with antiphon (Latin)

Kýrie eléison ("Lord, have mercy" in Greek)

Pater noster (the Lord's Prayer in Latin)

Collect (English)

Closing sentences with benediction (Latin)

You can see that all four of the necessary elements for an office are present, and that Latin has been retained for the hymn, the psalmody, and the *Nunc Dimíttis* canticle, while the confession, the Scripture reading, and the collect (prayer) are all chanted in English. (The ancient prayer *Kýrie eléison* is sung in Greek; later we will mention why this is done.)

You don't have to know Latin to sing chant, but if you would like some guidance on pronouncing Latin, see Appendix A. Appendix B gives tips on how to divide Latin words into syllables. And throughout this book, we give translations of the chants so you can read what the Latin words mean in English. Listening to the chants on the CD that accompanies this book, and following along with the chants will help you associate the sounds of Latin with the written words.

✕

Now let's discuss each of the elements of Compline in more detail.

Hymns

Christians are familiar with singing *hymns*. Hymns are poetic texts set to music. They made their appearance very early in Christian worship. Ambrose, bishop of Milan in the fourth century, wrote hymns and established their regular use in the Divine Office; some of his hymns are still in use today. Since chant notation was not invented until later, it is mainly the texts that survive from these early centuries, and not necessarily the tunes.

A Latin hymn has the same form as an English hymn, in that it uses the same tune for each verse of the poetry.

Antiphons and Psalms

An *antiphon* is a short Gregorian chant that precedes a psalm (taken from the book of Psalms) or a canticle (a reading taken from another book of the Bible). The purpose of an antiphon is to introduce the psalm or canticle that follows, both through its music and through its words. The antiphon is then repeated following the psalm as a way of summing up and reflecting on the verses just chanted.

The antiphons are generally composed of simple melodies that lead quite naturally into the corresponding psalm tone. Musically speaking, the antiphon prepares the ear for the sounds of the mode in which the psalm will be chanted. We will be learning about modes in more detail in chapter 8.

The text of the antiphon is also important, because it is usually a verse that reflects the message of the psalm that follows. By paying attention to the words of the antiphon, we are prepared to understand the meaning of the psalm we will be chanting.

At the Community of Jesus we use different Compline antiphons for different weeks in the month because they all carry the theme of nighttime rest under the watchful care of God and his angels. Here is one example:

Angelis suis Deus mandávit de te, ut custódiant te in ómnibus viis tuis.
God has given his angels charge of you to guard you in all your ways.

Short Lessons and Responses

The practice in many early Egyptian monasteries was for one person to read or chant, while the rest sat and listened. We have preserved this tradition in Compline because the Scripture reading is chanted by a single voice. This reading is from a brief biblical passage that expresses a theme related to the close of the day.

After listening for God to speak through the reading, we respond by using the verse and response. In *responsorial* chanting, a soloist sings the verse, and then all respond by singing a prescribed refrain. This form serves a practical purpose. In the early centuries when chant was an oral tradition, most monasteries had only a few trained cantors. In responsorial chanting, people can follow the lead of the cantor and still participate in the office. It is from this practice that we get our "modern" cantor.

In the traditional Compline response, we quote Jesus' own words to the Father as he hung on the cross: "into your hands . . . I commend my spirit"—words that many people pray before they sleep.

The Nunc Dimíttis

Canticles are scriptural poems or songs that are found in books of the Bible other than the Psalms. Benedict prescribed the use of two New Testament canticles. The first was the Song of Zechariah (Luke 1:68–79). This is usually called the *Benedíctus* and is sung at Lauds. The second was the Song of Mary (Luke 1:46b–55). This is usually called the *Magníficat* and is sung at Vespers. Within a few centuries, the Roman church added a third New Testament canticle—the Song of Simeon (Luke 2:29–32), also called the *Nunc Dimíttis* and sung at Compline.

According to Luke, God had revealed to Simeon that he would see the Messiah before he died. As Jesus was brought by his parents to the temple for the ritual presentation of their firstborn son, Simeon recognized who Jesus was. He took the infant in his arms and recited the words of this canticle:

> Sovereign Lord, as you have promised, you now dismiss your servant in peace. For my eyes have seen your salvation, which you have prepared in the sight of all people, a light for revelation to the Gentiles and for glory to your people Israel.

As with the chanting of the psalms, an antiphon *Salva nos, Dómine* (Save us, Lord) is sung before and after the chanting of the canticle. In this case, the text of the antiphon is a prayer based on Scripture, rather than a direct quote from Scripture.

Here is the text of this lovely prayer:

> Salva nos, Dómine, vigilántes, custódi nos dormiéntes, ut vigilémus cum Christo et requiescámus in pace.

> *Save us, Lord, while we keep vigil; keep us while we sleep, that we may watch with Christ and rest in peace.*

Closing Prayers

The final moments of Compline consist of prayers that begin with the cantor chanting *Kýrie eléison* (Lord, have mercy), followed by everyone chanting *Christe eléison, Kýrie eléison* (Christ, have mercy; Lord, have mercy). These are the only Greek words used in the office. This plea reminds us of the blind man who called out to Jesus as recorded in Mark 10:46–52. It is also a reminder that before Latin came into liturgical use in the West, Greek was the language of the early church's worship.

The Lord's Prayer follows. The cantor intones *Pater noster* (Our Father), and then everyone prays the words of the prayer silently until the last two petitions—*et ne nos indúcas in tentatiónem, sed líbera nos a malo* (and lead us not into temptation, but deliver us from evil). Here, the cantor chants the first petition and everyone else responds with the second petition. Praying the central part of the *Our Father* silently is an ancient tradition that comes from the early centuries of the Christian era when Rome was persecuting the church and only baptized Christians knew the Lord's Prayer. By publicly reciting only the first and last lines, the persecuted Christians preserved the secrets of the Christian faith.

The ending prayers continue with a final collect (a short prayer of the day), and a final benediction (a prayer of blessing). In the last words of the office, we pray for God's assistance for us and for all our "absent brethren."

VARIATIONS IN COMPLINE

We live in a world filled with repetitive events that give definition to our lives. The most basic, of course, are the most natural: day and night, weeks, months, years, and seasons of the year. Whether or not we are aware of it, repetition influences much of our lives, giving us an anchor with which to meet all that is uncertain and changing in our world.

As liturgy developed in the Christian church, it was natural that it would reflect these same cycles:

- the **daily** cycle of the Eucharist and the Liturgy of the Hours;
- the **weekly** cycle, beginning with Sunday;
- the **yearly** cycle of liturgical seasons;
- and the **yearly** cycle of saints' days.

Compline is the office that is least affected by liturgical cycles. Because Benedict designed it to be simple and consistent throughout the year, Compline provides a wonderful beginning place for learning to chant.

There are, however, some variations to keep in mind, based on the liturgical seasons of the church. For example, Easter is the focal point of the liturgical year—the central celebration around which everything else revolves. Lent is the forty-day period of preparation that leads to Easter, and the days of the Easter season continue for fifty days until Pentecost. The Christmas season has a similar pattern: Advent is the period of preparation, and the days of the Christmas season culminate in Epiphany and the Baptism of the Lord.

There is an ancient tradition according to which the word "Alleluia" is omitted from worship during the season of Lent. In a sense, we "fast" from using that word during those forty days. How joyful it is to again sing "Alleluia" when Easter arrives! To expand the celebration of the Easter season, "Alleluia" is added to almost every part of the office.

Therefore, in the opening sentences of Compline you will see that, during Lent, "Alleluia" is replaced by a different phrase. Conversely, during the Easter season, "Alleluia" is added in several places.

✗

As you sing Compline, you might also choose to change some things for a little variety. For instance, you might decide during Lent to chant the psalms without an antiphon, or to chant them using a different mode.

CHAPTER 8

CHANTING THE COMPLINE PSALMS

MODE 8

Now let's learn how these basic principles will assist us in chanting Compline. The chief "ingredient" in any Gregorian office is the psalmody—chanting the psalms. Whether we are chanting one of the main "pillar" offices of the day—Lauds or Vespers—or a shorter, simpler office such as Compline, the chosen psalms are the "heart" of that particular office.

The book of Psalms is based on Hebrew poetry. The most common form of Hebrew poetry is characterized by what is known as parallelism. That is, there are two halves within each verse, and each half says something closely related to the other half. The second half normally reinforces and gives added interpretation to the concept presented in the first half. Here is an example from Psalm 4, the first psalm used in Compline.

*I will lie down and sleep in peace, * for you alone, O Lord, make me dwell in safety.*

   If you turn to Appendix D, you will notice that the two halves of each Latin psalm verse are separated by an asterisk, just like the English verse printed above. This demarcation will play an important part in helping us chant the psalms.

   Another tool you will need is knowing how to pronounce the Latin. If you are not familiar with how to pronounce Latin words, you will find useful pronunciation tips in Appendix A and B.

   Finally, remember that the most basic form of chant consists of reciting a text on a single pitch, called the *reciting tone*. Every mode formula has a reciting tone, as well as places where the melody changes to tell us we have reached the end of each half of the verse. This change in tune also enables us to either lift up the words or set them down gently. Each mode has its own particular pattern. Let's start with Mode 8, the first mode we will encounter in the office of Compline.

MODE 8—FIRST AND SECOND HALVES

Because Hebrew poetry makes a statement in the first half of a verse, and then elaborates on that statement in the second half, each psalm verse has a first and second half, separated by an asterisk. Therefore, each mode formula has a first and second half as well. In chant, we put these two elements together. It may help to think of the tune as a pattern that needs to be laid on the text or "fabric" of the psalms.

Let's look at this verse from Psalm 4, shown with the tune for Mode 8. The first half of the psalm verse coincides with the first half of the mode formula. Notice the asterisk at the end of the first line. This is the landmark that tells you that you have reached the end of the first half, or the *mediant* of the verse.

First half

Et sci-tó- te quó-ni-am mi- ri- fi- cá- vit Dó-minus sanctum su-um;*

Second half

Dó-minus ex-áu-di- et, cum clamá-ve- ro ad e- um.

*Know that the Lord has set apart the godly for himself; *
the Lord will hear when I call to him.

DO is the reciting tone for Mode 8. Closer to the asterisk, the tune goes up on the *su* of *suum*, and back to DO on the last syllable of the word. A delightful phenomenon called the *lifted accent* occurs between the text and the music at this point. If you listen to the example on **TRACK 18** on the CD, you will hear that there is a subtle separation between the final word accent and the last syllable, almost as if it is being gently tossed up. This lifted accent occurs in the first half of every psalm verse in Mode 8 when the final word has two syllables.

Now look at the second half of the verse, and you will notice that the tune remains on the reciting tone through the *ve* of *clamávero*. Then it moves down on the syllable *ro*, followed by an up and a down on the remaining syllables, *ad eum*, until the end of the verse. Listen to **TRACK 19** on your CD to hear the entire verse sung.

You will also notice that there are large accent marks above the text and staff, marks that point out the last Latin word accent for each half of the verse. These accent marks are added as extra landmarks, because all the formulas for the eight church modes are based on either word accents or word syllables. (This will become clearer as we go along; you may wish to refer to Appendix B now for an explanation of the Latin word accent.)

If you look back at our example, you will see that in the first half of the verse, the tune goes up on the final word accent (*su* of *suum*). But in the second half, the tune begins to change two syllables before the final word accent. (The final word accent is the *e* of *eum*, and two syllables back from that point is the *ro* of *clamávero*.)

If we were to make a short summary of the Mode 8 formula for each verse of the psalm, it might look like this:

Mode 8 **(TRACK 20)**
First half: Move up on last accent.
Second half: Move down two syllables before the last accent.

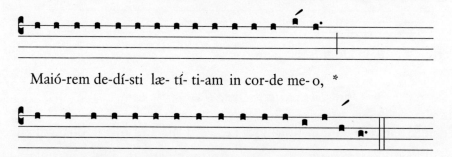

Maió-rem de-dí-sti læ- tí- ti-am in cor-de me- o, *

quam cum multi- pli-cántur fruméntum et vinum e- ó-rum.

*You have filled my heart with greater joy ***
than when their grain and wine and joy abound.

Using the mode formula above, we move up on the *me* of *meo* in the first half and down on the *num* of *vinum* in the second half, because we count back two syllables from the *ó* of *eórum* (the last accented syllable of the verse).

HOLLOW NOTES

Let's look at one more verse from the same psalm for another bit of information; in this verse we see two notes that are not filled in completely. These are called "hollow notes."

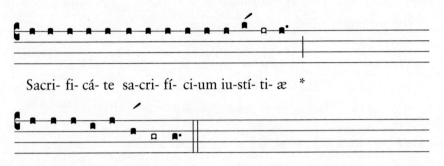

Sacri- fi- cá- te sa-cri- fí- ci-um iu-stí- ti- æ   *

et spe-rá- te in Dó-mi-no.

*Offer right sacrifices * and trust in the Lord.*

Notice that there are hollow notes toward the end of each half of the verse. There are two ways that Latin groups syllables. The two-syllable group is called a *spondee*, in which an accented syllable is followed by an unaccented one. The three-syllable group is called a *dactyl*, in which the accented syllable is followed by two unaccented ones. (You will find a further explanation of these terms in Appendix B. You may wish to refer to this appendix before continuing with this chapter.)

Hollow notes show us what note to chant when the final word is a dactyl. The two final words in the verse above, *iustítia* and *Dómino*, are both dactyls, so we need the hollow notes in order to chant the verse properly. We use these hollow notes any time the ending of the first half of a psalm verse or the ending of the second half of a psalm verse involves a dactyl. (There is one more place where we might encounter a hollow note, and that is at a "flex"—we will explain the flex in the next section of this chapter.)

If you listen to **TRACK 21** on your CD, you can hear this last verse chanted to Mode 8. Chant along with the example and notice how naturally the Latin words fit the tune.

THE FLEX

Sometimes one half of a line of chant is quite long, so it is divided into two parts. At the end of the first segment there is a dagger (†), which is called a *flex*. The flex signals us to drop down from the reciting note DO to LA on the final syllable (the final two syllables if the word is a dactyl) before the dagger. The flex is another reminder that chant is sung speech. Just as we would indicate a comma by lowering our voice a bit, so we indicate a sung comma by chanting a lower pitch. Look at the example below from Psalm 91 and listen to it on **TRACK 22** on your CD to hear how the flex is sung in Mode 8.

Dicet Dó*mino*: † «Refúgium meum et fortitúdo **mé**a, * Deus meus, sperá***bò*** in eum».

*I will say of the Lord, "He is my refuge and my fortress, * my God, in whom I trust."*

In this example we've used bold italics to show the syllables that drop down from the reciting tone at the flex. We've used bold to show the syllable in the first half at which the voice goes up in pitch, and to show the syllable in the second half at which the voice goes down.

MARKING MODE 8 PSALMS

In the service of Compline in Appendix E we have the text of the psalms without the tune shown in the previous examples. Remember that we begin each psalm verse on the reciting note. It is important when learning to chant that we have some way of marking when to move away from the reciting tone, according to the formula for Mode 8. People who sing chant often use a light pencil mark in their chant music to show when to move up or down in pitch. Here is one way we could mark the verse we have been considering.

Et scitóte quóniam mirificávit Dóminum sanctum súum; *
Dóminus exáudiet, cum clamávero ad eum.

*Know that the Lord has set apart the godly for himself; **
the Lord will hear when I call to him.

In the first half, an upward slash has been added on the last accent because the tune moves up at this point. In the second half, a downward slash has been added where the tune goes down—two syllables before the last accent. It is possible to be more detailed in the second half and show where the tune goes down, then back up, and then down again:

Dóminus exáudiet, cum clamávero ad eum.
The Lord will hear when I call to him.

You might find a method that works better for you. Whatever method you use, marking the verses ahead of time makes it easier to sing the psalms properly.

Using the information you have just learned about how to mark psalms, you may wish to try marking the psalms for Mode 8 in the service of Compline in Appendix E—using light pencil marks so you can correct them easily if you make a mistake. After you try marking these psalms, check your answers against the Answer Key in Appendix D.

CHAPTER 9

CHANTING THE COMPLINE PSALMS

MODES 8g AND 3a

✖

EUOUAE

Let's continue our study of psalmody, looking again at Mode 8. Each of the modes has only one tune for the first half of each verse, but there can be a variety of tunes for the second half. These different endings are given letter names to distinguish them. Since the tune we looked at in the last chapter uses the "g" ending, it is called Mode 8g. Let's look again at this ending, using the last two words of the *Glória Patri* verse.

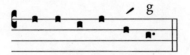

sæ- cu- ló-rum. A-men.

This ending is called the final cadence.

Now, consider what the ending, or final cadence, of Mode 8g would look like if only the vowels of "sæculórum—Amen" were given.

E u o u a e

We find this ending, with only the vowels listed, placed at the end of every antiphon as an aid to show the final cadence. Now look at the antiphon *Angelis suis*, found on page 98, and locate the final cadence with the Euouae letters. There is the ending for Mode 8g. These vowels give us another piece of important information: they tell us what the reciting tone is. The first note of the ending is always the reciting tone of any mode. This "shorthand" collection of letters, Euouae, gives us much of the information we need to know for chanting the psalms.

MODE 3a

In the last chapter we learned how to mark the Compline psalms for Mode 8. Toward the end of Compline (just before the final prayers), we find the Canticle of Simeon, the *Nunc Dimíttis*. Take a moment to read the text for the *Nunc Dimíttis* in Appendix E on page 106, and you will see that it is a fitting prayer to end the day.

The *Nunc Dimíttis,* one of three New Testament Canticles sung at the end of offices, is encompassed by a beautiful antiphon that gives a light, buoyant effect, because of the lifted accents in the melody. Listen for this when you hear the *Nunc Dimittis,* found on **TRACK 23** on the CD. If you look above the capital "S" of the antiphon shown on page 105, you will see that the *Nunc Dimíttis* is chanted in Mode 3, with ending "a." Mode 3a moves according to a rule involving two accents. Remember that Mode 8 moved up on the last accent before the mediant, and it moved down two syllables before the last accent at the final cadence. By contrast, Mode 3 moves up on the next-to-last accent, and it does this for both halves of the verse. Let's take a look at the final verse of the *Nunc Dimíttis.*

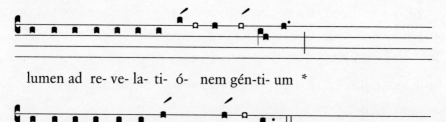

lumen ad re- ve- la- ti- ó- nem gén-ti- um *

et gló-ri- am ple-bis tu-   æ Is- ra- el.

*[A] light for revelation to the Gentiles *
and for glory to your people Israel.

We can surmise that the reciting tone is likely to be TI, since the majority of the notes fall on the space beneath the top line. (And for Mode 3, TI is the reciting tone!)

Mode 3a: First Half

In the first half of the verse, the accent marks above the staff indicate that the tune moves up at the next-to-last accent on the *ó* of *revelatiónem.* In this example, we can see how the tune fits the words. Now let's go through the process step by step.

If we look at these words alone: *revelatiónem géntium,* the first thing we do is to find the last accent, that is, the *gén* of *géntium.* This is the final accent in the first half of the verse. As we see in the example, the syllable *gén* is placed under the last accent over the staff. Because *géntium* is a dactyl—having three syllables—we need to use the hollow note of our ending. (If the last word were a spondee, we would not use the hollow note, but we would pair the word accent with the high-low notes—the clivis. We will explain more about this later.)

Still looking only at the words and continuing to move left, we look for the next-to-last word accent, and we find it on *ó* of *revelatiónem.* Again, we can check our musical example of this verse and find the accent mark above the *ó.* This accent mark coincides with the first rise in the music from the reciting tone, TI, to RE. This is another example of how the text is lifted up by the melody of the psalm tones.

Mode 3a: Second Half

Now we can apply the same rules to marking the second half of the verse. Here is our example once again:

lumen ad re- ve- la- ti- ó- nem gén-ti- um *

et gló- ri- am ple-bis tu-   æ Is- ra- el.

*[A] light for revelation to the Gentiles *
and for glory to your people Israel.*

The melody moves on the next-to-last accent in this half also, as shown by the accents above the staff. Look at the following words: *plebis tuae Israel.* We see that the last accent is on *Is* of *Israel.* If we go back to the left, we find the next-to-last accent on the *tu* of *tuae.*

MORE ABOUT HOLLOW NOTES

As we saw earlier, Mode 3a gives us the opportunity to use the hollow notes of the mode formula if the words are dactyls. Let's look at the first verse of the *Nunc Dimíttis.*

Nunc di-mít-tis servum tu- um, Dó-mi-ne, *

secúndum verbum tu-um in pa-   ce,

*Now you dismiss your servant, Lord, ***
according to your word, in peace.

Walking through the process of figuring out where to move, the formula
is this:

Mode 3
First half: Move up on next-to-last accent
Second half: Move up on next-to-last accent

First, we find the final accent in the first half of the verse:
The *Do* of *Dómine* fits with the pattern that has a hollow note on
the pitch DO. It is followed by a high-low (clivis) on the pitches TI–
LA. This is where we will sing the syllable *mi* of *Dómine*, followed by
a single note on the final syllable, *ne*. Now what if our last word were
mei? We need only the TI–LA clivis followed by the final DO if the
last word is a spondee. For this reason, there is a bracket above these

notes, indicating that the notes used depend on whether the word is a dactyl (three syllables) or a spondee (two syllables). The accent mark shifts accordingly.

Here are examples from the first half of each of the first two verses of the *Nunc Dimíttis*. The first half of the first verse ends with a three-syllable group (a dactyl); the first half of the second verse ends with a two-syllable group (a spondee):

First half of first verse

Nunc di-mít-tis servum tu- um, Dó-mi-ne, *

First half of second verse

qui- a vi- dérunt ó-cu-li   me- i *

Since *Dómine* has three syllables, the hollow note is used to sing the syllable *Dó*. But since *mei* has two syllables, the hollow note is not used. Now look at the next-to-last accent of the first half of the first verse: since *tu* of *tuum* has two syllables, we do not need to use the hollow note that follows the syllable *tu* of *tuum*. But since *óculi* has three syllables, we do use the hollow note to sing the syllable *cu* of *óculi*.

The same procedure applies to the second half of the verses. Hollow notes are needed only with groups of three syllables. Listen to the first two psalm verses of the *Nunc Dimíttis* on **TRACK 23** of the CD, you will hear how natural it sounds to use the hollow note for a dactyl and not to use it for a spondee.

Mode 3 has a more ornate mode formula than Mode 8. That is, there are more notes to sing on some of the syllables than in Mode 8. In fact, in the first half of the third verse of the *Nunc Dimíttis,* you will find that there are only two words, with a total of four syllables. There are not enough syllables to chant both the reciting tone and the mediant formula, so we begin that particular verse on the note where the next-to-last accent is found.

Although you have been working through some technical material in this chapter, when you listen to the *Nunc Dimíttis* on **TRACK 23**, you will see how beautifully the words are lifted up with this graceful melody. As you listen, you may want to follow the words of the *Nunc Dimíttis* in Appendix E so you can hear and see the text at the same time. This will help you associate the sounds with the written words as you chant Compline yourself.

CHAPTER 10

THE SHAPE OF THE MELODIC LINE IN PSALMODY

✖

In the last several chapters we have covered the technical material that we need in order to chant the psalms.

Now it is time to remind ourselves that the beauty of chant is in its simplicity. The rhythm of the parallel verses, paired with the psalm tones that highlight the text, can serve to both calm and energize our spirits.

Above all, the words should be treated with care. When we chant the psalms, we must use our true voice, with the tempo of each word and phrase being the same as though it were spoken.

If we were to make a pictorial version of a chanted psalm verse, it might look like this.

First half   *   Second half

The first half of each verse starts gently, with a sense of forward motion to the cadence. Once the final accent has been reached, the tone softens as we release the last syllable of the word in an upward direction.

At this point, where the asterisk separates the two halves of the psalm verse, there is a slight pause. The purpose of the pause is to let the sound die away. This should not be unnaturally long, unless we are chanting in a space that produces a lot of reverberation. This pause also enables us to contemplate briefly what we have just chanted, before we launch into the second half of the verse. During the pause, it sometimes helps if we say silently, "one-two," or we might think of the notes we have just sung. Another way to time the pause is to silently say *Glória Patri*. During this time, we want to take a good breath. This intake of breath, while we are mentally saying one of these aids, is an important part of the rhythm of the psalmody.

At the beginning of the second half of the verse, we start at the volume level at which we left off, and again we warm the verse as it moves toward its final accents.

One of the unique aspects of this way of chanting the psalms is that the pause occurs at the mediant, not at the end of the verse, as we might expect. The next verse begins immediately at the same volume as the ending of the previous verse. This is what gives the psalmody its ebb and flow.

If you are chanting the psalms by yourself, you will need to take a quick breath at the end of each verse, but take your bigger breath at the mediant. If you are chanting in a group, you can sing alternate verses and "hand them back and forth" to each other. This also enables you to employ a good intake of breath while the other side is completing their final cadence, so you can gently pick up at the volume at which they have left off.

TONUS IN DIRECTUM

In previous chapters we have learned how to chant Psalms 4, 91, and 134 in Mode 8, using an appropriate antiphon. They can also be chanted without an antiphon using a special tone called *Tonus in Directum*. *Tonus in Directum* is the simplest of all the psalm tones, and the oldest, and it begins on the reciting tone. At the mediant cadence, we move down two syllables before the final accent (much as we did for the second half of the verse in Mode 8). In the second half, we stay on the reciting tone for the remainder of the verse.

Look at the following example, using the first verse of Psalm 91. Follow along with **TRACK 24** on the CD.

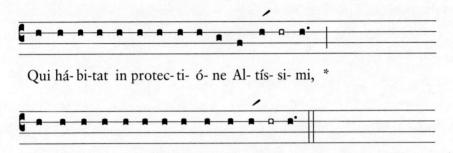

Qui há- bi-tat in protec-ti- ó- ne Al- tís- si- mi, *

sub umbra Omni-potén-tis commo- rá- bi-tur.

*He who dwells in the shelter of the Most High ****
will rest in the shadow of the Almighty.

DO is both the reciting tone and the home tone. This simple tone uses only three pitches: DO, TI, and LA.

You may find that you prefer chanting Compline using *Tonus in Directum* for all three psalms. You might also want to alternate using that version with the one using the antiphon and Mode 8. The Community of Jesus uses various antiphons throughout the year. During the season of Lent, we switch to the simpler *Tonus in Directum* and omit the antiphon.

A LIVING CONVERSATION

✖

Wherever you sing chant—in your office, in your living room, in your car—you are joining a company of pilgrims who are speaking to God and listening for his voice.

Chant, by its very nature, consists as much in listening as it does in chanting. Whether you are chanting by yourself as you listen to a CD, or especially if you are chanting with a group of people, listening is the key for staying together and moving as one voice. If you are chanting with a group, you should not chant so loud that you cannot hear your neighbors. On the other hand, your chanting should not be so soft that it hides your sound, so that it cannot be heard at all. In short, you must use your true voice!

Latin is an eloquent language when spoken well. Latin is also a wonderful language for chanting because of its inherent lilt in the arrangement of accented and unaccented syllables. Since there is never an accent on a final syllable, all of the phrases conclude with a sense of being lifted up with grace.

Above all, the dialogue—one that takes place between God and ourselves—is the essential purpose of the Divine Office. We endeavor to chant well because we endeavor to pray well. Gregorian chant, then, is a language of the prayerful heart. It is poetry of praise in word and song.

NOTES

�֍

1 Dom Jacques Hourlier, *Reflections on the Spirituality of Gregorian Chant* (Brewster, MA: Paraclete Press, 1995), 46.

2 *Plainchant for Everyone*, Royal School of Church Music Handbook No. 3, Mary Berry (RSCM, 1979), 3.

3 Dom Louis Soltner, *Solesmes and Dom Guéranger*, tr. Joseph O'Connor (Brewster, MA: Paraclete Press, 1995), 108.

4 Hourlier, *Reflections on the Spirituality of Gregorian Chant*, 9.

5 Taken from the Lutheran Concordia Theological Seminary's Web page, http://www.ctsfw.edu/chapel/index.php.

6 George Guiver, CR, *Company of Voices: Daily Prayer and the People of God* (New York: Pueblo Publishing Co., 1988), 7, 36.

APPENDICES

HOW TO PRONOUNCE LATIN

✗

The Latin used in Gregorian chant is not the classical language used by Cicero. Just as English has changed since the time of Shakespeare, the pronunciation of Latin has changed over a period of centuries. As the Roman Empire broke into many smaller countries, local languages began to replace Latin in common speech. However, Latin remained the language of scholarship, and the Western church continued to use Latin in religious services such as the Eucharist and the Divine Office.

Here are some guides for pronunciation:

VOWELS

Vowels are always pronounced the same:
> **a** as in father: *Pater, ángelus*
> **e** as in prey: *Dómine, exáudi*
> **i** as in the vowel sound in sea: e.g. *benedícat, Dóminus*

o as in r**o**pe (without the diphthong): *sperábo, orémus*

u as in r**u**de: *Spíritus, refúgium*

y is pronounced the same as **i** (that is, it has the vowel sound of s**ea**): *kýrie*

æ and **œ** are pronounced like the Latin letter **e** (that is, the sound of the "e" of pr**ey**): *cælis, cœna*

DIPHTHONGS

In some words, we find two vowels together that form only one syllable, but the sound of each vowel is heard distinctly. These are called *diphthongs*. The diphthongs in church Latin are *au* and *eu*.

au is pronounced much like the "ow" of **ow**l or c**ow**: *lauda, exaudívit*

eu is pronounced much like the separate vowels put together quickly, sounding much like "AAY-ooo" in English: *euge, heu*

CONSONANTS

Most consonants sound as they do in English. Here are some exceptions:

c sounds like **k** before **-a, -o** and **-u**: *cadent, cum, corde*

However, **c** sounds like **tch** before **-e** and **-i**: *decem, sacrifícium, incípit*

ch always sounds like **k**: *Christo, chérubim, chorus*

g sounds like the first **g** of garage or gorge before **-a, -o** and **-u**: *singuláriter, synagóga*
However, **g** sounds like the second **g** of garage or gorge before **-e** and **-i**; it is more like dj: *ángelis, refúgium*

h is always silent: *hábitat, adhǽsit*

Exceptions: There are two words in which you will need to make a **k** sound instead of the **h**: mihi (pronounced "MEE-kee") and nihil (pronounced "NEE-keel").

ph is always **f**: *Pháraoh*

r is always rolled, like the **r** of Spanish or Italian: *refúgium, liberábit, loríca*

s is always pronounced as in English "see" and never has a "z" sound as in English "roses": *Deus, spe, requiéscam*

th is pronounced like **t** alone (because **h** is always silent): *thesáuris, thronum*

i at the beginning of a word can be used as a consonant. It sounds like **y** in English: *Iesus, Ioseph, iurávit*

HOW TO DIVIDE LATIN WORDS INTO SYLLABLES

✕

It is easy to divide Latin words into syllables if we follow this simple rule: the number of syllables equals the number of vowels or diphthongs (which are two vowels pronounced as one syllable).

If there are two consonants together, divide between them: *mit-te, il-lum*

If there is a vowel followed by a consonant and a vowel, divide after the first vowel: *Pa-tri, Ie-sus, cho-rus*

If two vowels come together and are not diphthongs, divide between them: *tu-um, fí-li-i*

GROUPS OF TWO SYLLABLES (SPONDEE)

Part of the rhythmic sense of Latin comes from the fact that the accents fall every two or every three syllables. In a two-syllable word, the pattern is always this:

accent / non-accent

examples: *Patri, sancto*

This arrangement of two syllables, with the first one accented, is called a **spondee**.

If a word has three or more syllables, and the accent falls on the second to last syllable, you still have this same pattern, with a non-accented preparatory syllable.

examples: *portábunt, peccatórum*

GROUPS OF THREE SYLLABLES (DACTYL)

Or, the accent can be on the first of three syllables, creating this pattern:

accent / non-accent / non-accent

examples: *Spíritus, Dóminus*

This arrangement of syllables is called a **dactyl**.

It is easy to remember the difference between these two terms if you know that "dactyl" is the Greek word for "finger." Just as a finger has three segments, a chant dactyl has three syllables. (In French, typing on a keyboard is called *dactylographie*, literally meaning "writing with the fingers.")

This also holds true for words of more than three syllables that have this pattern:

examples: *conquiéscite, singuláriter*

THE LATIN WORD ACCENT

The principal accent of a Latin word is high, light, and brief:

high: The pitch of the accented syllable is slightly higher than that of the surrounding syllable(s).

light: The accented syllable is buoyant, not stressed or emphasized by putting pressure in the voice.

brief: The accented syllable is not drawn out; rather, it is quite rapid.

WRITTEN ACCENT MARKS IN LATIN

In words of three syllables or more, an accent mark is written above the accented syllable. This helps us know which syllable is set apart.

LIFTED ACCENTS

A lifted accent is a light, subtle separation between the final word accent and the last syllable, almost as if it is being gently tossed up. A lifted accent occurs in chant when both of the following are true:

1.   The principal accent of a Latin word appears on a **single pitch**; and
2.   The syllable **after** the principal accent has either:
     a) a lengthening on the note, shown either by a dot or an episema (little line over the note), OR
     b) has multiple notes.

See the examples below, taken from the antiphon for the *Nunc Dimíttis*. There is an explanation of how to chant the lifted accent on page 56. Lifted accents occur in psalmody, as well as in antiphons and hymns.

Here is one example of a lifted accent, when the accent is followed by a lengthening **(TRACK 25)**:

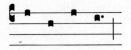

dor-mi- **én**- tes

Here is another example of a lifted accent, when the accent is followed by multiple notes **(TRACK 26)**:

Chri-sto

ANSWER KEY: MODES

✕

Page 31: Make a square note for each consecutive space and line, heading in an upward diagonal to the right, and then write the solfège names underneath each note:

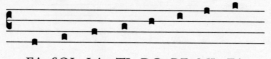

FA SOL LA TI DO RE MI FA

Page 34: Mark the half steps with carets on a scale that begins with FA:

FA SOL LA TI DO RE MI FA

Page 35: Mark the half steps with carets on a scale that begins with DO:

DO RE MI FA SOL LA TI DO

Page 36: Mark the half steps with carets on a scale that begins with RE:

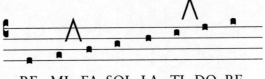

RE MI FA SOL LA TI DO RE

Page 37 : Mark the half steps with carets on a scale that begins with MI:

MI FA SOL LA TI DO RE MI

Page 37: Mark the half steps with carets on a scale that begins with FA:

FA SOL LA TI DO RE MI FA

Page 37: Mark the half steps with carets on a scale that begins with SOL:

SOL LA TI DO RE MI FA SOL

ANSWER KEY: MARKING THE PSALMS

✖

Mark the three Compline psalms for Mode 8. The psalms are marked using the following system:

First half: the next-to-last syllable, on which our voices go up, is in bold and has an acute accent mark, like this—á.

Second half: the second-to-last syllable before the last accent, on which our voices go down, is in bold and has a grave accent mark, like this—à. (The grave accent mark is not used in Latin; it is used here only to show that our voices go down on the syllable containing the grave accent.)

Where there is a flex, indicated by a dagger (†), our voices go down from DO to LA on the syllable or syllables marked in **_bold italics_**.

PSALM 4

Cum invocárem, exáudívit me Deus iustítiae **mé**æ. * In tribulatióne dila**tà**sti mihi;

miserére m**é**i * et exáudi orati**ò**nem meam.

Fílii hóminum, úsquequo gravi **cór**de? * Ut quid dilígitis vanitátem et qu**æritì**s mendácium?

Et scitóte quóniam mirificávit Dóminus sanctum **sú**um; * Dóminus exáudiet, cum clamáve**rò** ad eum.

Irascímini et nolíte peccá**re** † loquímini in córdibus **vé**stris, * in cubílibus vestris et **còn**quiéscite.

Sacrificáte sacrifícium iustítiae * et sperá**tè** in Dómino.

Multi dicunt: «Quis osténdit nobis **bó**na?» * Leva in signum super nos lumen vultus **tùi**, Dómine!

Maiórem dedísti lætítiam in corde **mé**o * quam cum multiplicántur fruméntum et vi**nùm** eórum.

In pace in idípsum dórmiam et requi**é**scam, * quóniam tu, Dómine singuláriter in spe con**stì**tuísti me.

Glória Patri et **Fí**lio, * et Spirí**tùi** Sancto,

sicut erat in princípio et nunc et **sém**per * et in saécula sæcu**lò**rum. Amen.

PSALM 91

Qui hábitat in protectióne Al**tís**simi, * sub umbra Omnipoténtis **còm**morábitur.

Dicet Dó**mino**: † «Refúgium meum et fortitúdo **mé**a, * Deus meus, sperá**bò** in eum».

Quóniam ipse liberábit te de láqueo ve**nán**tium * et a ver**bò** malígno.

Alis suis obumbrábit ti**bi**, † et sub pennas eius con**fú**gies; * scutum et loríca vé**rì**tas eius.

Non timébis a timóre noctúrno, a sagítta volánte in di*e*, † a peste perambulánte in **té**nebris, * ab extermínio vastánte **ìn** merídie.

Cadent a látere tuo mil**le** † et decem mília a dextris **tú**is; * ad te autem non ap**prò**pinquábit.

Verúmtamen óculis tuis conside**rá**bis, * et retributiónem pecca-tó**rùm** vidébis.

Quóniam tu es, Dómine, refúgium **mé**um. * Altíssimum posuísti habitácù**lum** tuum.

Non accédet ad te **má**lum, * et flagéllum non appropinquábit tabernácù**lo** tuo,

quóniam ángelis suis mandábit **dé** te, * ut custódiat te in ómnibus **vì**is tuis.

In mánibus por**tá**bunt te, * ne forte offéndas ad lápidem **pè**dem tuum.

Super áspidem et basilíscum ambu**lá**bis * et conculcábis leónem **èt** dracónem.

Quóniam mihi adhǽsit, liberábo **é**um; * suscípiam eum, quóniam cognóvit **nò**men meum.

Clamábit ad me, et ego exáudiam e*um*; † cum ipso sum in tribu-latió**ne**, * erípiam eum et glorificà**bo** eum.

Longitúdine diérum replébo **é**um * et osténdam illi salu**tà**re meum.

Glória Patri . . .

PSALM 134

Ecce benedícite Dóminum, omnes servi **Dó**mini, * qui statis in domo Domin**ì** per noctes.

Extóllite manus vestras ad sanctuárium * et benedíc**ì**te Dóminum.

Benedícat te Dóminus ex **Sí**on, * qui fecit cæ**lùm** et terram.

Glória Patri . . .

COMPLINE

✄

The recording of Compline **(TRACK 1)** *is for Monday of Week 1. However, we have included here the Office of Compline with the varying hymns, antiphons, Scriptures, and prayers for Monday through Friday, Weeks 1 through 4, for your reference and use.*

OPENING SENTENCES

Versicle

O God, come to my assistance.

Response

O Lord, make haste to help me.
Glory be to the Father, and to the Son,
and to the Holy Spirit. As it was in
the beginning, is now, and always will
be, forever and ever. Amen. Allelúia.

Versicle

Deus, in adiutórium meum inténde.

Response

Dómine, ad adiuvándum me festína.
Glória Patri, et Fílio, et Spirítui Sancto.
Sicut erat in princípio, et nunc, et
semper, et in sǽcula sæculórum.
Amen. Allelúia.

CONFESSION

I confess to God Almighty, the Father, the Son, and the Holy Spirit, that I have sinned in thought, word, and deed through my own grievous fault. Wherefore, I pray God to have mercy on me. Almighty God, have mercy upon us, forgive us all our sins and deliver us from all evil; confirm and strengthen us in all goodness, and bring us to life everlasting; through Jesus Christ our Lord. Amen.

ABSOLUTION

May the almighty and merciful Lord grant to us pardon and remission of all our sins, time for amendment of life, and the grace and comfort of the Holy Spirit. Amen.

Weeks I and III

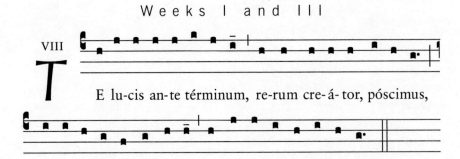

VIII

TE lu-cis an-te términum, re-rum cre-á-tor, póscimus,

ut só-li- ta clemén-ti- a sis præsul ad cu-stó-di-am.

To you before the end of light, Creator of all things, we beg that,
with your usual compassion, you would be a protector to guard us.

May our hearts dream of you,	Te corda nostra sómnient,
sense your presence in deep sleep	te per sopórem séntiant,
and always sing your glory	tuámque semper glóriam
with the approaching light.	vicína luce cóncinant.
Grant us a wholesome life,	Vitam salúbrem tríbue,
revive our zeal, our love;	nostrum calórem réfice
let your brightness light up	tætram noctis calíginem
the awful darkness of the night.	tua collústret cláritas.
Grant this, O Father Almighty,	Præsta, Pater omnípotens,
through Jesus Christ the Lord,	per Iesum Christum Dóminum,
who with you for all time	qui tecum in perpétuum
reigns with the Holy Spirit. Amen.	regnat cum Sancto Spíritu. Amen.

Weeks II and IV

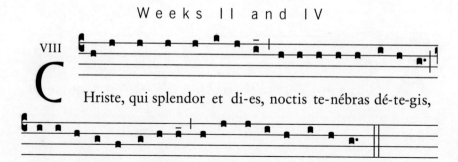

VIII

Christe, qui splendor et di-es, noctis te-nébras dé-te-gis,

lu-císque lumen créde-ris, lumen be- á- tis prǽdi-cans,

O Christ, you who are splendor and day, who lay bare the shadows of the night,
you are faithful, O light of light, proclaiming light to the blessed,

We pray, holy Lord,
that you keep us this night;
may our rest be in you;
grant us quiet hours.

While our eyes are given sleep,
may our hearts always keep vigil toward you;
and protect with your right hand
the faithful, who love you.

Our defender, look on us,
repel those who are lying in wait,
direct your servants
whom you bought with your blood.

To you, O Christ, king most loving,
and to the Father be glory,
with the Spirit, the Paraclete,
for everlasting ages. Amen.

Precámur, sancte Dómine,
hac nocte nos custódias,
sit nobis in te réquies,
quiétas horas tríbue.

Somno si dantur óculi,
cor semper ad te vígilet;
tuáque dextra prótegas
fidéles, qui te díligunt.

Deténsor noster, áspice,
insidiántes réprime,
gubérna tuos fámulos,
quos sánguine mercátus es.

Sit, Christe, rex piíssime,
tibi Patríque glória,
cum Spíritu Paráclito,
in sempitérna sǽcula. Amen.

Week I

A.VIII g

AN- ge-lis su-is * Deus mandá- vit de te,   ut cu-stó-diant te in ómnibus vi-is tu-is.   E u o u a e.

God has given his angels charge of you to guard you in all your ways.

Week II

A.VIII g

IN pa- ce * in id- í-psum dórmi-am et requi- éscam.

E u o u a e.

In peace I will both sleep and rest.

Week III

A.VIII g

QUI há-bi-tat * in ad- iu-tó-ri- o Al- tís- si- mi, in protec-ti- ó- ne De- i cæ- li commo-rá- bi-tur.   E u o u a e.

He who dwells in the shelter of the Most High, will abide under the protection of the God of heaven.

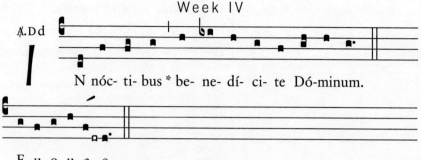

Week IV

A.Dd

I N nóc- ti- bus * be- ne- dí- ci- te Dó-minum.

E u o u a e.

In the night, bless the Lord.

PSALMS

PSALM 4

Thanksgiving

The resurrection of Christ was God's supreme and wholly marvelous work (St. Augustine).

Answer me when I call to you O my righteous God. Give me relief from my distress;

be merciful to me and hear my prayer.

How long, O men, will you turn my glory into shame? How long will you love delusions and seek false gods?

Know that the lord has set apart the godly for himself; the Lord will hear when I call to him.

Cum invocárem, exaudívit me Deus iustítiæ meæ. * In tribulatióne dilatásti mihi;

miserére mei * et exáudi oratiónem meam.

Fílii hóminum, úsquequo gravi corde? * Ut quid dilígitis vanitátem et quǽritis mendácium?

Et scitóte quóniam mirificávit Dóminus sanctum suum; * Dóminus exáudiet, cum clamávero ad eum.

In your anger do not sin; when you are in your beds search your hearts and be silent.

Offer right sacrifices and trust in the Lord.

Many are asking, "Who can show us any good?" Let the light of your face shine upon us, O Lord.

You have filled my heart with greater joy than when their grain and wine and joy abound.

I will lie down and sleep in peace, for you alone, O Lord, make me dwell in safety.

Glory be to the Father and to the Son, and to the Holy Spirit.

As it was in the beginning, is now, and always will be forever and ever. Amen.

Irascímini et nolíte peccáre; † loquímini in córdibus vestris, * in cubílibus vestris et conquiéscite.

Sacrificáte sacrifícium iustítiæ * et speráte in Dómino.

Multi dicunt: «Quis osténdit nobis bona?» * Leva in signum super nos lumen vultus tui, Dómine!

Maiórem dedísti lætítiam in corde meo, * quam cum multiplicántur fruméntum et vinum eórum.

In pace in idípsum dórmiam et requiéscam, * quóniam tu, Dómine, singuláriter in spe constituísti me.

Glória Patri, et Fílio, et Spirítui Sancto.

Sicut erat in princípio, et nunc, et semper, et in sǽcula sæculórum. Amen.

PSALM 91

Under the protection of the most high

I have given you authority to tread upon snakes and scorpions (Luke 10:19a).

He who dwells in the shelter of the Most High will rest in the shadow of the Almighty.

I will say of the Lord, "He is my refuge and my fortress, my God in whom I trust."

Surely he will save you from the fowler's snare and from the deadly pestilence.

He will cover you with his feathers, and under his wings you will find refuge; his faithfulness will be your shield and rampart.

You will not fear the terror of night, nor the arrow that flies by day, nor the pestilence that stalks in the darkness, nor the plague that destroys at midday.

A thousand may fall at your side, ten thousand at your right hand, but it will not come near you.

You will only observe with your eyes and see the punishment of the wicked.

Qui hábitat in protectióne Altíssimi, * sub umbra Omnipoténtis commorábitur.

Dicet Dómino: † «Refúgium meum et fortitúdo mea, * Deus meus, sperábo in eum».

Quóniam ipse liberábit te de láqueo venántium * et a verbo malígno.

Alis suis obumbrábit tibi, † et sub pennas eius confúgies; * scutum et loríca véritas eius.

Non timébis a timóre noctúrno, a sagítta volánte in die, † a peste perambulánte in ténebris, * ab extermínio vastánte in merídie.

Cadent a látere tuo mille † et decem mília a dextris tuis; * ad te autem non appropinquábit.

Verúmtamen óculis tuis considerábis, * et retributiónem peccatórum vidébis.

If you make the Most High your dwelling—
even the Lord, who is my refuge—

then no harm will befall you, no
disaster will come near your tent.

For he will command his angels concerning
you to guard you in all your ways;

they will lift you in their hands, so that you
will not strike your foot against a stone.

You will tread on the lion and the cobra;
you will trample the great lion and the
serpent.

"Because he loves me," says the Lord, "I
will rescue him; I will protect him, for he
acknowledges my name.

He will call upon me, and I will answer him;
I will be with him in trouble, I will deliver
him and honor him.

With long life will I satisfy him and show
him my salvation."

Glory be to the Father and to the Son, and
to the Holy Spirit.

As it was in the beginning, is now, and
always will be forever and ever. Amen.

Quóniam tu es, Dómine, refúgium
meum. * Altíssimum posuísti
habitáculum tuum.

Non accédet ad te malum, * et
flagéllum non appropinquábit
tabernáculo tuo,

quóniam ángelis suis mandábit de te, *
ut custódiant te in ómnibus viis tuis.

In mánibus portábunt te, * ne forte
offéndas ad lápidem pedem tuum.

Super áspidem et basilíscum
ambulábis * et conculcábis leónem
et dracónem.

Quóniam mihi adhǽsit, liberábo
eum; * suscípiam eum, quóniam
cognóvit nomen meum.

Clamábit ad me, et ego exáudiam eum;
† cum ipso sum in tribulatióne, *
erípiam eum et glorificábo eum.

Longitúdine diérum replébo eum *
et osténdam illi salutáre meum.

Glória Patri, et Fílio, et Spirítui
Sancto.

Sicut erat in princípio, et nunc, et
semper, et in sǽcula sæculórum. Amen.

PSALM 134

Evening prayer in the temple

Praise our God, all you his servants, you who fear him, small and great (Revelation 19:5b)!

Praise the Lord, all you servants of the Lord who minister by night in the house of the Lord.

Lift up your hands in the sanctuary and praise the Lord.

May the Lord, the Maker of heaven and earth, bless you from Zion.

Glory be to the Father and to the Son, and to the Holy Spirit.

As it was in the beginning, is now, and always will be forever and ever. Amen.

Ecce benedícite Dóminum, omnes servi Dómini, * qui statis in domo Dómini per noctes.

Extóllite manus vestras ad sanctuárium * et benedícite Dóminum.

Benedícat te Dóminus ex Sion, * qui fecit cælum et terram.

Glória Patri, et Fílio, et Spirítui Sancto.

Sicut erat in princípio, et nunc, et semper, et in sǽcula sæculórum. Amen.

SHORT LESSONS

Monday

1 Thessalonians 5:9-10

For God has not destined us for wrath, but to obtain salvation through our Lord Jesus Christ, † who died for us so that whether we wake or sleep * we might live with him.

Response: Thanks be to God!

Tuesday

1 Peter 5:8-9

Be sober, be watchful. Your adversary the devil prowls around like a roaring lion, seeking some one to devour. † Resist him, firm in your faith, * knowing that the same experience of suffering is required of your brotherhood throughout the world.

Response: Thanks be to God!

Wednesday

Ephesians 4:26-27, 31-32

Be angry but do not sin; do not let the sun go down on your anger, and give no opportunity to the devil. † Let all bitterness, wrath, anger, clamor and slander be put away from you, with all malice, * and be kind to one another, tenderhearted, forgiving one another, as God in Christ forgave you.

Response: Thanks be to God!

Thursday

1 Thessalonians 5:16-18, 23

Rejoice always, pray constantly, give thanks in all circumstances; for this is the will of God in Christ Jesus for you. † May the God of peace himself sanctify you wholly; * and may your spirit and soul and body be kept sound and blameless at the coming of our Lord Jesus Christ.

Response: Thanks be to God!

Friday

Jeremiah 14:9b, 21, 22b

You are among us, O Lord, and we bear your name; do not forsake us! † For the sake of your name do not despise us: do not dishonor your glorious throne. * Remember your covenant with us and do not break it. Our hope is in you.

Response: Thanks be to God!

VERSICLE AND RESPONSE

Versicle

Into your hands, Lord, I
commend my spirit.

Response

You have redeemed us, Lord,
O God of truth.

Versicle

In manus tuas, Dómine,
comméndo spíritum meum.

Response

Redemísti nos, Dómine,
Deus veritátis.

GOSPEL CANTICLE

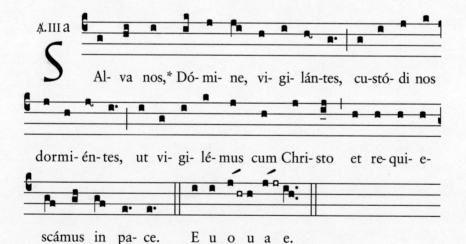

℣. III a

S Al- va nos,* Dó- mi- ne, vi- gi- lán-tes, cu-stó- di nos

dormi- én-tes, ut vi- gi- lé- mus cum Chri-sto et re-qui-e-

scámus in pa- ce. E u o u a e.

Save us, Lord, while we keep vigil; keep us while we sleep,
that we may watch with Christ and rest in peace.

LUKE 2:29-32
Christ, the Light of the Gentiles and the Glory of Israel

"Sovereign Lord, as you have promised, you now dismiss your servant in peace.

For my eyes have seen your salvation,

which you have prepared in the sight of all people,

a light for revelation to the Gentiles and for glory to your people Israel."

Glory be to the Father . . .

Nunc dimíttis servum tuum, Dómine, * secúndum verbum tuum in pace,

quia vidérunt óculi mei * salutáre tuum,

quod parásti * ante fáciem ómnium populórum,

lumen ad revelatiónem géntium * et glóriam plebis tuæ Israel.

Glória Patri . . .

CLOSING PRAYERS

Versicle
   Lord, have mercy.
Response
   Christ, have mercy.
   Lord, have mercy.

Our Father . . . *silently until*

Versicle
   And lead us not into temptation.
Response
   But deliver us from evil.

Versicle
   Lord, listen to my prayer.
Response
   And let my cry come to you.

Let us pray.

Versicle
   Kýrie eléison.
Response
   Christe eléison.
   Kýrie eléison.

Pater noster . . . *silently until*

Versicle
   Et ne nos indúcas in tentatiónem.
Response
   Sed líbera nos a malo.

Versicle
   Dómine, exáudi oratiónem meam.
Response
   Et clamor meus ad te véniat.

Orémus.

COLLECTS

Monday

Send your peace into our hearts, O Lord, at the evening hour, † that we may be contented with your mercies of this day, and confident of your protection for this night; * and now, having forgiven others, even as you forgive us, † may we have a pure comfort and healthful rest under the shadow of your wings. We ask this through our Lord Jesus Christ, your Son, who lives and reigns with you and the Holy Spirit; one God for ever and ever.

Response: Amen.

Tuesday

Visit this place, O Lord, and drive far from it all snares of the enemy; † let your holy angels dwell with us to preserve us in peace; * and let your blessing be upon us always. We ask this through our Lord Jesus Christ, your Son, who lives and reigns with you and the Holy Spirit; one God for ever and ever.

Response: Amen.

Wednesday

Lord Jesus Christ, you have given your followers an example of gentleness and humility, † a task that is easy, a burden that is light. * Accept the prayers and work of this day, † and give us the rest that will strengthen us to render more faithful service to you. Who live and reign with the Father and the Holy Spirit; one God for ever and ever.

Response: Amen.

Thursday

Be present, O merciful God, † and protect us through the hours of this night, * so that we who are wearied by the changes and chances of this life † may rest in your eternal changelessness. We ask this through our Lord Jesus Christ, your Son, who lives and reigns with you and the Holy Spirit; one God for ever and ever.

Response: Amen.

Friday

Keep watch, dear Lord, with those who work, or watch, or weep this night, † and give your angels charge over those who sleep. * Tend the sick, Lord Christ; give rest to the weary, bless the dying, soothe the suffering, pity the afflicted, shield the joyous; † and all for your love's sake. We ask this through our Lord Jesus Christ, your Son, who lives and reigns with you and the Holy Spirit; one God for ever and ever.

Response: Amen.

Versicle

Lord, listen to my prayer.

Response

And let my cry come to you.

Versicle

Dómine, exáudi oratiónem meam.

Response

Et clamor meus ad te véniat.

BENEDICTION

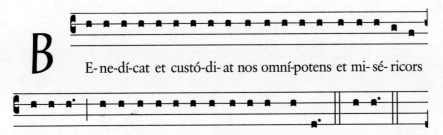

B E- ne-dí-cat et custó-di- at nos omní-potens et mi- sé- ricors

Dóminus, * Pa-ter, et Fí- li- us, et Spí-ri-tus Sanctus.   Amen.

*May the almighty and merciful Lord bless us and keep us,
the Father, the Son and the Holy Spirit. Amen.*

Versicle

May divine help always remain with us.

Response

And with our absent brethren. Amen.

Versicle

Divínum auxílium máneat semper nobíscum.

Response

Et cum frátribus nostris abséntibus. Amen.

SELECT GLOSSARY

Chant: Also known as Gregorian chant, refers to a form of melodic singing, unaccompanied, with biblical or liturgical texts developed in the early Christian church primarily between the years AD 800 and 1200.

EUOUAE: An abbreviation for "sæculorum, amen" which shows the primary vowel of each syllable. This abbreviation of the final two words of the Gloria Patri is placed at the end of an antiphon underneath pitches on a staff showing the ending melodic formula of the given chant mode. It is not actually chanted at the end of the antiphon but acts only as a guide for how to chant the end of a psalm verse.

Mode: The general name given to the pitches used in a given chant—similar to the term "scale" in modern music.

Neume: The general name given to a note or note groups in chant notation.

Office: The term often applied to the various services of chanted prayers and Scriptures (such as Lauds, Vespers, or Compline).

Pope Gregory I ("the Great") *(590-604)*: the Pope from whom the name "Gregorian" is taken in reference to the chant. Numerous stories have arisen over the centuries attributing the composition of many chants to this Pope. Though there is little reliable evidence to support those stories, this Pope did pave the way in the early church for the development of liturgical music, likely having created a singing school for the education of musicians.

Solesmes: The Abbey of St. Peter of Solesmes (France) has, since the early nineteenth century, been the primary place for the historical research and restoration of Gregorian chant through the research of scholars such as Dom Eugene Cardine. You might find a visit to their website of interest (www.solesmes.com) as much detail is offered about the chant.

Versicle and **Response**: These terms are used in the various office prayers. *Versicle* indicates a line chanted by an individual and *Response* indicates a line chanted by the congregation.

TRACK LISTING
FOR THE ACCOMPANYING CD
TO *THE SONG OF PRAYER*

✕

TRACK 1	The Full Service of Compline sung by the Community of Jesus	14:42
TRACK 2	Compline Antiphon: *Salva Nos*	:37
TRACK 3	The Do to Do scale	:30
TRACK 4	Example of Do Ti Do	:17
TRACK 5	Example of Do Ti La Ti Do and Do La Do	:27
TRACK 6	The Fa to Fa scale	:32
TRACK 7	The Re to Re scale	:32
TRACK 8	The Mi to Mi scale	:28
TRACK 9	The Sol to Sol scale	:34
TRACK 10	Example of Mode 1	:28
TRACK 11	Example of Mode 2	:26
TRACK 12	Example of Mode 3	:26
TRACK 13	Example of Mode 4	:26
TRACK 14	Example of Mode 5	:23
TRACK 15	Example of Mode 6	:27
TRACK 16	Example of Mode 7	:26
TRACK 17	Example of Mode 8	:28
TRACK 18	Example of a lifted accent	:21
TRACK 19	Full verse in Mode 8, *Et scitote . . .*	:28
TRACK 20	Full verse in Mode 8, *Majorem dedisti . . .*	:28
TRACK 21	Full verse in Mode 8, *Sacrificate sacrificium . . .*	:27
TRACK 22	Example of a flex	:26
TRACK 23	Compline Canticle *Nunc Dimittis* with Antiphon	2:01
TRACK 24	Example of Tonus in Directum	:26
TRACK 25	Example of a lifted accent when followed by a lengthening	:20
TRACK 26	Example of a lifted accent when followed by multiple notes	:49

ABOUT PARACLETE PRESS

Who We Are

Paraclete Press is a publisher of books, recordings, and DVDs on Christian spirituality. Our publishing represents a full expression of Christian belief and practice—from Catholic to Evangelical, from Protestant to Orthodox.

We are the publishing arm of the Community of Jesus, an ecumenical monastic community in the Benedictine tradition. As such, we are uniquely positioned in the marketplace without connection to a large corporation and with informal relationships to many branches and denominations of faith.

What We Are Doing

Books

Paraclete publishes books that show the richness and depth of what it means to be Christian. Although Benedictine spirituality is at the heart of all that we do, we publish books that reflect the Christian experience across many cultures, time periods, and houses of worship. We publish books that nourish the vibrant life of the church and its people—books about spiritual practice, formation, history, ideas, and customs.

We have several different series, including the best-selling Paraclete Essentials and Paraclete Giants series of classic texts in contemporary English; Voices from the Monastery—men and women monastics writing about living a spiritual life today; award-winning poetry; best-selling gift books for children on the occasions of baptism and first communion; and the Active Prayer Series that brings creativity and liveliness to any life of prayer.

Recordings

From Gregorian chant to contemporary American choral works, our music recordings celebrate sacred choral music through the centuries. Paraclete distributes the recordings of the internationally acclaimed choir Gloriæ Dei Cantores, praised for their "rapt and fathomless spiritual intensity" by *American Record Guide*, and the Gloriæ Dei Cantores Schola, which specializes in the study and performance of Gregorian chant. Paraclete is also the exclusive North American distributor of the recordings of the Monastic Choir of St. Peter's Abbey in Solesmes, France, long considered to be a leading authority on Gregorian chant.

Videos

Our videos offer spiritual help, healing, and biblical guidance for life issues: grief and loss, marriage, forgiveness, anger management, facing death, and spiritual formation.

Learn more about us at our website:
www.paracletepress.com, or call us toll-free at 1-800-451-5006.

SCAN TO READ MORE

This collection of Gregorian Chant books and CDs represents the most authentic scholarship and worship in the field of Gregorian chant today. All are available through Paraclete Press.

Gregorian Chant: A Guide to the History and Liturgy
Dom Daniel Saulnier, OSB, Translated by Dr. Mary Berry, CBE
Trade paper, $19.99

Offers a fascinating tour through chant's historical and musical origins, showing the role that it plays in the history and liturgy of the Western church.

Reflections on the Spirituality of Gregorian Chant
Dom Jacques Hourlier
Trade paper, $14.99

A spiritual work that reflects on characteristics of Gregorian chant that have attracted the attention of so many: its permanence, beauty, and history, as well as its liturgical, sacred, and philosophical qualities.

An Overview of Gregorian Chant
Dom Eugène Cardine
Trade paper, $14.99

Solesmes monk Dom Eugène Cardine (1905-1988) uncovered the elusive secrets of Gregorian rhythm, thus revealing some of the original beauty of Chant. In this volume, he sums up the origin, decline and restoration of chant, challenging others to continue his work.

The Parish Book of Chant, Second Edition

Hardcover, $20.00

This 320-page volume contains a complete order of Mass for both the Ordinary and the Extraordinary Form of the Roman Rite in side-by-side Latin and English, an expanded Kyriale, Sequences, litanies, Communion Propers, full chant hymn verses, ribbons, tutorial, and the fully and updated Ordo to both forms of the Mass.

Gregorian Missal

Hardcover, $35.95

This 700-plus page handbook is all you or your schola needs for singing the Mass on all Sundays and principal feasts.

Graduale Triplex

Hardcover, $64.95

This 900-plus page resource includes the Roman Gradual, with the addition of the early neumatic notation from two early manuscripts (St. Gall printed in red; Laon printed in black) as well as the current chant notation found in the *Graduale Romanum*.

Solesmes and Dom Guéranger, 1805-1875

Dom Louis Soltner

Trade paper, $24.99

Today's liturgical renewal owes a great debt to Dom Guéranger, who re-founded the Abbey of St. Peter of Solesmes and guided the spiritual growth that led to their renowned scholarship in the field of Gregorian chant.

Visit www.chantresources.com for the complete collection of books and CDs from the Monks of Solesmes and the Gloriæ Dei Cantores Schola, including chant books for the Mass and the Liturgy of the Hours (Missals, Antiphonales, Kyriales, etc.).

Also, you can connect with a Gregorian chant specialist at Paraclete Press by email (musicinfo@paracletepress.com) or by joining our Gregorian chant Facebook group.

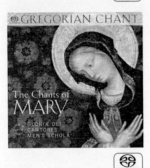

The Chants of Easter

GDCD 126, 978-1-61261-381-9, $16.95

The Feast of the Resurrection, rooted in the earliest centuries of Christian worship, is the "celebration of celebrations" reflected in the chants on this recording— including the Propers of Easter Day and Gregorian chants for the octave of Easter.

The Chants of Christmas

GDCD 125, 978-1-61261-377-2, $16.95

Gregorian chant lifts us out of the ordinary stresses of life and invites us to contemplate the timeless and unchanging love of God. *The Chants of Christmas* presents some of the most beautiful Gregorian chants, including the Christmas Day Mass.

*"Allow this CD to transport you
right past the malls and into
the season's sacred mystery."*
—THE DALLAS MORNING NEWS

"Three of the finest chant CDs have been released by Gloriæ Dei Cantores:
The Chants of Angels, The Chants of Mary, *and* **The Chants of the Holy Spirit.**
*Put a Gloriæ Dei Cantores SACD on your surround sound stereo and be
transported to a timeless place of eternal beauty."*
—KANSAS CITY STAR

The Coming of Christ

GDCD 033, 978-1-55725-310-1, $16.95

The Coming of Christ is the first of a series of three CDs using the exquisite music of Gregorian chant to describe and illuminate the life of Christ. Well-known pieces alternate with numerous antiphons to bring us closer to the time of Christ's birth and early childhood. The prophetic announcements, the longing and anticipation of Christ's birth, as well as the joy of the angels' message are all vividly portrayed in the chant.

The Beloved Son

GDCD 032, 978-1-55725-296-8, $16.95

The Beloved Son, the second recording in the series, celebrates the public life and ministry of Christ through well-known chants and brief antiphons.

I Am With You

GDCD 034, 978-1-55725-321-7, $16.95

Christ's Passion, the ultimate sacrifice, is the subject of *I Am With You*, the third disc, which includes the chanted Passion narrative according to the Gospel of John, featuring three cantors who assume the characters in the story of the Passion. This stirring music evokes the passion, mystery, and beauty of the life of Christ.

Gloriæ Dei Cantores Schola was honored to work with guest conductor Dr. Mary Berry, CBE, founder of the Schola Gregoriana in Cambridge, England, in recording these CD's.

Gregorian Requiem

GDCD 117, 978-1-55725-519-8, $16.95

The Requiem Mass, one of the most frequently performed Masses of the Medieval period, is included here with antiphons for the vigil prior to the funeral, antiphons chanted in the church, and the sequence *Dies irae, dies illa,* best known for its inclusion in more modern requiems such as those by Mozart, Verdi, and Duruflé. Thus, this recording presents a medieval funeral Mass as it would have been chanted in the fourteenth century.

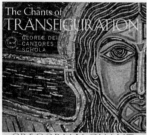

The Chants of Transfiguration

GDCD 127, 978-1-61261-417-5, $16.95

Full of joy and hope, this recording includes the chants of the prophecies of the Transfiguration, chants that tell the story of Christ's Transfiguration, and chants that highlight the possibility and promise of our own transfiguration. Beautiful, chant-inspired organ works bookend the program.

GLORIÆ DEI CANTORES SCHOLA is dedicated to the singing and study of Gregorian chant. Its expertise and experience come from daily chanting of the Liturgy of the Hours as well as the Ordinary and Proper of the Mass at the Church of the Transfiguration. The Schola also conducts chant workshops and performs in concert with Gloriæ Dei Cantores. Years of study with the late Dr. Mary Berry, CBE, founder of the Schola Gregoriana in Cambridge, England, and the monks of St. Peter's Abbey, Solesmes, France, also contributes to the Schola's passion for Gregorian chant as a vibrant and living form of sung prayer.

These CDs and others are available at bookstores everywhere,
or call Paraclete Press at 1-800-451-5006 or visit www.paracletepress.com.

The recordings of Gloriae Dei Cantores Schola are also available as
digital download through iTunes, eMusic, Rhapsody, www.nativedsd.com,
and a number of other digital music services.